They like it best when you say nothing at all

Keeping our heads down can mean that hard-won rights can easily be lost. Sometimes we choose to stay quiet, but often we are complicit without realising, says **Rachael Jolley**

49(01): 1/3 I DOI: 10.1177/0306422020917592

"**I**T IS EASY to part with or give away great privileges, but hard to be gained if once lost," said Quaker William Penn, who went on to establish the state of Pennsylvania in the USA.

Far more recently, another wise man, former Lord Chief Justice of England and Wales Lord Judge, said: "There are still many countries in the world where what we happily call our rights remain privileges waiting to be won and entrenched."

These thoughts are the cornerstones of the theme of this issue – the idea that we can give away our rights if we do not stand up for them.

We can be complicit in letting them erode if we feel they are not important enough or let other things take precedence, and many are willing to give away freedom for security.

The Merriam Webster dictionary tells us that the root of the English word "complicit" comes from the Latin word "complicare", meaning "to fold together", and that it has evolved over time into meaning helping to do wrong or to commit a crime in some way – in other words, letting ourselves be folded into a bad idea.

In allowing ourselves to be complicit, we potentially allow those in power to take away some of our rights forever.

As Lord Judge also points out in his book The Safest Shield, we should be careful never to assume that liberties, rights and justice can be taken for granted.

Complicity is our theme for today because, in 2020, there are multiple powers that like us to give things away – our privacy, our knowledge and even our power to say no. They try to get us to fold into their purpose, to agree it and let them move forward.

It comes at us in many forms.

Many of us are complicit in giving away lots of information about ourselves, such as our contacts and photo albums from our phones. We do this in exchange for free use of software apps – Facebook or Google Maps, for instance.

We do a deal with their owners that they will let us use their stuff, and not charge us, but all along, deep down, we probably guess there is some pay-off.

We know there's no such thing as a free lunch, so why would there be free email or free software? The answer is: there isn't. There is a price to pay – you exchange your knowledge and contacts for that which is "free". And, as Mark Frary investigates on p31, taking →

EDITOR-IN-CHIEF
Rachael Jolley
DEPUTY EDITOR
Jemimah Steinfeld
SUB EDITORS
Tracey Bagshaw,
Adam Aiken

CONTRIBUTING EDITORS
Kaya Genç (Turkey),
Laura Silvia Battaglia
(Yemen and Iraq),
Stephen Woodman
(Mexico)

EDITORIAL ASSISTANT
Orna Herr
ART DIRECTOR
Matthew Hasteley
COVER
Ben Jennings

ASSOCIATE EDITOR
Mark Frary
MAGAZINE PRINTED BY
Page Bros.,
Norwich UK

INDEX ON CENSORSHIP
indexoncensorship.org I +44 (0) 20 3848 9820 I 1 Rivington Place, London EC2A 3BA, United Kingdom

Supported by

ARTS COUNCIL
ENGLAND

some decisions – such as being logged in all the time – means you are giving away more than you might imagine.

Frary tracks how much information Google is storing about him and his movements, and realises that it knows 700 places which he has visited in the past six years. That's a lot of knowledge about him, his movements and where he might be going.

It doesn't take much imagination to think back to a time when that would be a treasure trove to a government wanting to know more about its citizens because it wanted to prevent them having information, passing it to others and knowing what was going on.

Let's take the Latin American dictatorships of the 1970s and 1980s, for instance, where journalists and many others were "disappeared" for asking the wrong questions.

What if that kind of information had been available to those governments? What extra power would it have given them to track down dissenters and to send in the police?

Shift forward in time to Venezuela today, from where Stefano Pozzebon reports for us on why the media and activists feel afraid. Threats and imprisonment are being used by the authoritarians in charge of this troubled nation to silence those who disagree with them.

And that government could try to access individuals' whereabouts from Google Maps simply by putting in a request to Google. The company doesn't always hand over information to governments which request it, but many times it does. Imagine for a moment what that might feel like.

Pozzebon said: "For those who don't want to join the almost five million Venezuelans who have already left, not saying anything about anything becomes the only way to cope."

When we are afraid we are most at risk from the pressure that others might place on us not to speak out or criticise. We can be complicit in attempts by the powerful to change society and remove those rights that Penn set out.

Of course, acting out of fear is understandable. It is easy for those far away who are not risking their lives, or those of their families, to say: "Oh you must do this, or stand up for that." It is not so easy to do that once you know what, and whom, you put at risk.

This desire to quiet your anger and put it away until a less dangerous time is something that most humans can understand.

That's why Kaya Genç's article from Turkey is so important. In it he describes the moment that changed one academic's attitude dramatically. The name of Anıl Özgüç, a professor of medicine at Istanbul's Aydın University, was added to a pro-government petition without her knowledge. The petition said she demanded the imprisonment of scholars who had signed a "Peace Petition". The thing was, she didn't.

And by that action, her attitude – which had been to keep quiet and hope for the best – changed.

She had reached her tipping point and she was no longer prepared to shut up: it was a step too far to take her name from her. Like John Procter in The Crucible, giving up her name was too much.

Suddenly she put aside her fears and spoke up. She is now an open critic of the government's attempts to restrict academic freedom.

This chimes with new research from Jennifer Pan, at Stanford University, who looks at repression in authoritarian countries. She found that arrests of outspoken activists in Saudi Arabia had the effect of silencing the individuals but, surprisingly, did not deter others from speaking out. In fact, it motivated more people to criticise the government and the monarchy,

The petition said she demanded the imprisonment of scholars who had signed a 'Peace Petition'. The thing was, she didn't

and stepped up calls for change. So while outsiders might expect the opposite to be true – that people would be cowed – Pan's research shows that there is a tipping point and it can prompt more outspoken calls for change.

Complicity is not an easy topic. We should all be able to see there are sometimes reasons for not challenging the powerful, and times when it would be understandable to feel afraid or at risk. Many around the world take that responsibility very seriously, and choose to make brave choices – even when it might put them in danger. It is these people whom Index often profiles, and we are in awe of those who can be incredibly brave when the odds are stacked against them.

Complicity is a challenge for us constantly, and in small and large ways we will be confronted by it all our lives. The question is: what is our response?

Rachael Jolley is editor-in-chief of Index

ABOVE: A protester dressed as the Statue of Liberty attends a protest in Central, Hong Kong

CONTENTS

VOLUME 49 NUMBER 01 – SPRING 2020

COMPLICITY

Why and when we choose to censor ourselves and give away our privacy

CREDIT: Ben Jennings

IN FOCUS

CULTURE

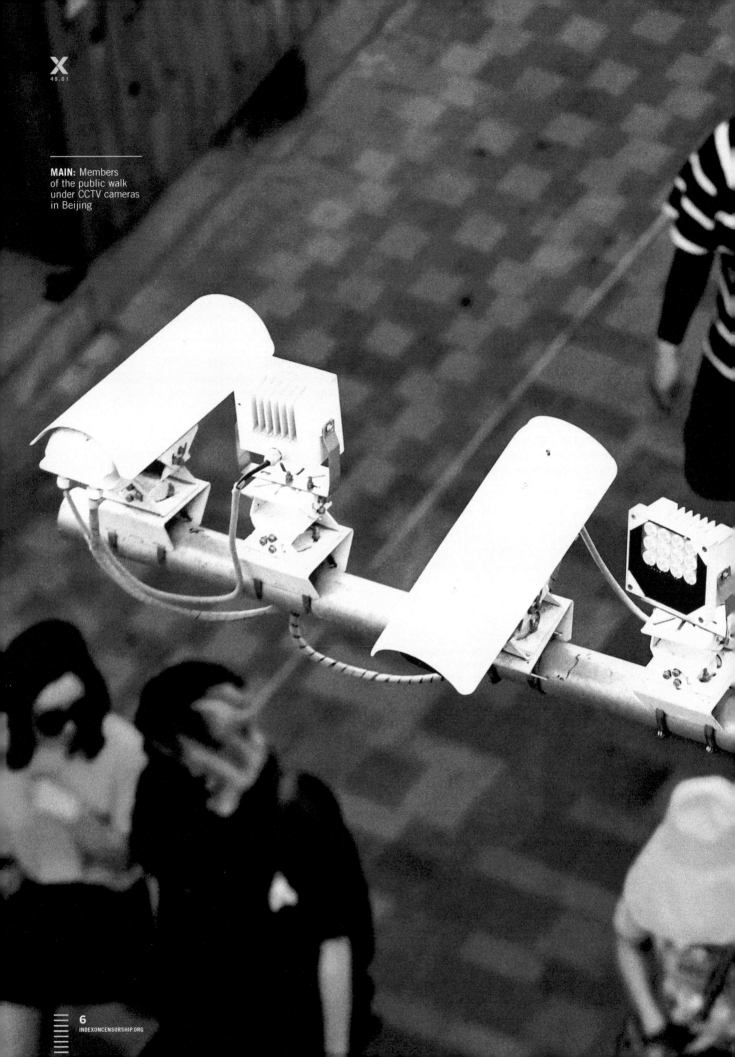

MAIN: Members of the public walk under CCTV cameras in Beijing

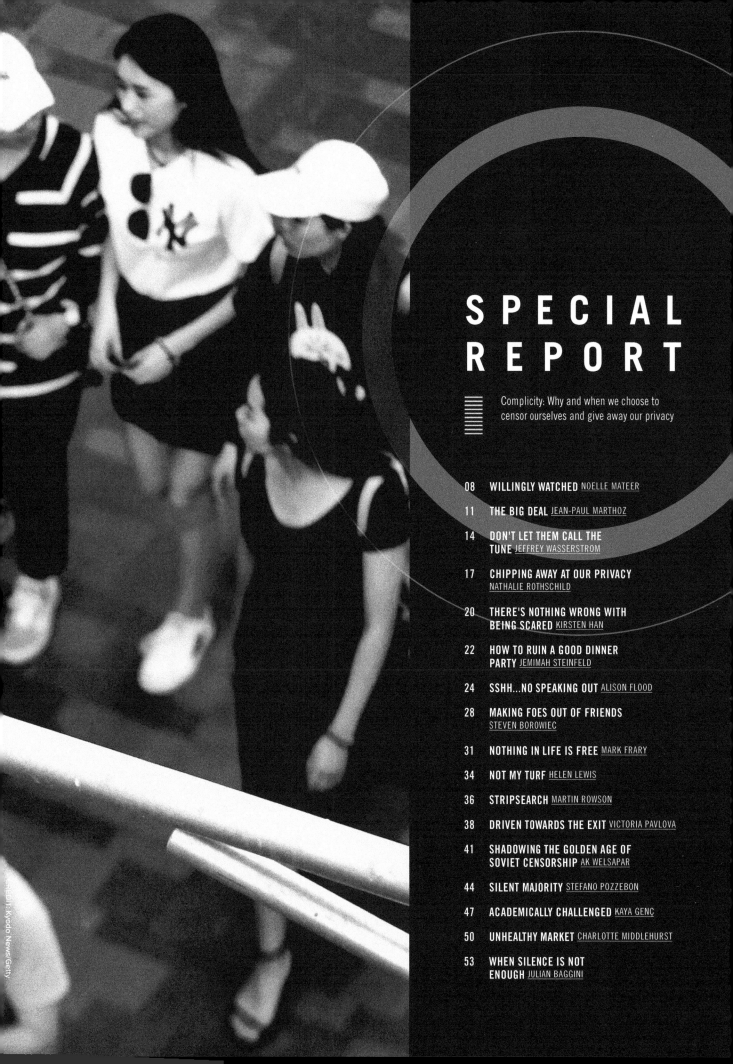

SPECIAL REPORT

Complicity: Why and when we choose to censor ourselves and give away our privacy

Willingly watched

People all over China are embracing CCTV cameras in the name of security without considering the implications for their free speech. **Noelle Mateer** finds out why

49(01): 8/10 I DOI: 10.1177/0306422020917593

I WAS SURPRISED WHEN I returned home from work to find my landlord installing a prison-like panel of metal bars over my bedroom window. The room, which had a lockable door, was inside our courtyard apartment, also lockable. Bars on top of this seemed absurd to me, given Beijing's already low levels of crime. But my landlord thought otherwise.

"It's because of the tourists," he said, referring to the throngs on Ghost Street, a nearby strip of restaurants popular with visitors. "Someone could climb over the roof and get in the courtyard." He made a convoluted gesture meant to resemble a ninja-like intruder getting through. He then showed me the new security camera he'd placed outside the outer door, its lens pointing down at the doorstep as if to leer at all the mailmen, pizza delivery guys or roommates' boyfriends who wished to enter.

My landlord – and his fluffy dog, Tiger – once watched over the apartment himself. But that changed in 2017 when Beijing authorities conducted one of the most sweeping construction drives in years, euphemistically dubbed a "beautification campaign". Shop doors were bricked over, second storeys were torn down and whole alleys of buildings were given a fresh new brick layer of uniform grey. Not coincidentally, the renovations resulted in thousands of people moving out of the *hutongs* (lanes), my landlord included. Authorities tore down his apartment at the front of our courtyard and he moved out of the home he had lived in for decades into a tall, austere concrete building.

The campaign stripped the once-bustling *hutongs* down to their bare, brick-walled essentials. But it did add one thing: more CCTV cameras.

In 2015, Beijing authorities announced that every major street corner in the capital was monitored. Now, government-installed cameras are so plentiful that, if you squint, *hutongs* look like they're adorned with the gargoyles of Notre Dame. According to Oliver Philippou, a senior analyst at IHS Markit, which specialises in expertise on global technologies, China's installed surveillance cameras surged by nearly 70% in recent years to 350 million in 2018, up from 210 million in 2015.

"By 2021, China's installed base is expected to rise to 490 million cameras," Philippou said. "Driven by the government's Xue Liang programme [the nationwide drive to unite the country's various CCTV cameras under a unified surveillance network], the Chinese market receives significantly more government funding than any other region in the world with the aim of providing widespread video surveillance coverage within public areas."

By 2021, China's installed base is expected to rise to 490 million cameras

Despite the implications this has on free expression in a country that is one of the most censored in the world – and mounting evidence of how it is already being deployed against Muslims in the province Xinjiang (internet experts revealed in 2019 that a surveillance company was tracking the movements of at least 2.5 million residents there as part of a far-reaching security clampdown) – people still want more cameras. In China, as with the rest of the world, consumer video devices are a growing market, Philippou notes, though, proportionally speaking, that the consumer market for these devices isn't as large as it is in the USA. What's different is that, in China, consumer demand has surged alongside government-led surveillance pushes. Chinese tech companies are marketing sleek, easily installable home cameras; Xiaomi sells a popular security camera for as little as $30, which users can sync with an app and watch live footage while they're away.

My landlord was just one of many in my neighborhood who complemented our *hutong*'s new cameras with his own. After all the small shops and noodle joints were cleared out, the only businesses that repopulated our *hutong* were higher-end boutique hotels, selling the traditional *hutong* experience to visitors from cities in China where ancient alleyways no longer existed. These upscale businesses came with their own, gleaming cameras.

The *hutongs* are quieter now, but their chatty noise was once its own kind of security. Before CCTV cameras, nosy neighbours and shopkeepers were a de facto neighbourhood watch. (I know this from experience: An utterly terrifying woman who lived across from me

Xiaomi sells a popular security camera for as little as $30, which users can sync with an app and watch live footage while they're away

used to make me pick up rubbish in the street, even though it was never mine.) This old-fashioned security network harks back to a time before the block housing developments which dominate Chinese cities today and are staffed 24/7 by omniscient *bao'ans* (security guards). In *hutongs*, the people hanging out on their doorsteps playing mahjong or drinking tea were the security.

Peter Hessler references this in his 2006 New Yorker essay about living off Ju'er Hutong, just two blocks west of mine, when he calls "hanging around in the street with the neighbours" the "ultimate hutong sport". He then notes the omniscience of nosy neighbours when he wonders how a local matchmaker knew of his Italian heritage – she'd heard it from the bike repairman on his street. "I had no memory of the conversation, but I picked up a valuable *hutong* lesson: never underestimate how much the bike repairman knows."

More recently, China Unicom referenced the power of neighbours in an advert for its 5G services, in which a group of grannies sitting around outside recognise someone unusual in their neighbourhood and stop crime using

ABOVE: CCTV in the Forbidden City, Beijing

BIG BROTHER IS WATCHING

Just how is surveillance used in China? **Orna Herr** lists five examples

CORONAVIRUS DRONES
The Chinese authorities have been using surveillance technology to monitor and control the population during the coronavirus outbreak. Audio-equipped drones are hovering over residential streets telling citizens it sees without facemasks to go indoors.

SUBDUING THE UYGHURS IN XINJIANG
The surveillance system in Xinjiang, western China, is being used as part of an extreme crackdown on the Uyghur Muslims. Among other measures, technology is targeting Uyghurs to help assess who should be sent to "re-education camps" and monitoring them upon release.

PHONE DETECTION
In April 2019, The New York Times found that in one apartment complex in Zhengzhou facial recognition cameras, combined with technology that can identify mobile phone numbers, matched 3,000 numbers with faces in just four days.

PYJAMA SHAME
In the city of Suzhou, the authorities published photos of people wearing pyjamas in the street to publicly shame them for "uncivilised behaviour". Facial recognition technology was used to capture the images and identify them.

SEVEN MINUTES
BBC reporter John Sudworth teamed up with the police in Guiyang, southwest China, to find out how long it would take for them to locate and apprehend him using surveillance technology. The answer? Seven minutes.

→ their phones.

Renovations dampened this streetside conviviality, injecting an air of distrust into the once-friendly neighbourhoods. Fortunately, it lives on elsewhere. I am currently based in the south-western city of Kunming, where government reach is less visible and the march of modernisation feels slower than in Beijing. By the entrance to my apartment block is a small shop. The shopkeeper, Mr Li, and I are friendly – he likes to ask about what Americans eat for dinner, and more than once he has let me know that there was chilli sauce on my shirt.

Recently, police arrived at our compound's front gate, responding to a noise complaint. Whoever had called in had said the foreigner was having a loud party, probably because expats in China have a well-earned reputation for partying. When the police asked about the foreigner in the compound, Li vouched for me, saying I was well-behaved. He was right. When the police knocked on my door I was in my pyjamas, washing dishes, and they apologised for disturbing me. But what would have happened if I wasn't well behaved? In China, badly behaved can mean anything from criminal activity to simply saying or writing the wrong thing about the government. It's hard to go under the radar when we're all being watched.

In Beijing's *hutong* renovation campaign, small shops like Li's were the first to go, the Lis of their respective blocks replaced with cameras. What happens in Beijing is a template for the rest of China. Soon it is likely that we will all be watched and much the worse for it. ⊗

Noelle Mateer works at the Chinese publication Caixin. She is based in Yunnan, south-west China

The big deal

Jean-Paul Marthoz investigates the relationship between French journalists and those in power – and what is not being covered

49(01): 11/13 I DOI: 10.1177/0306422020917594

FRENCH JOURNALISTS LIKE quoting Albert Londres (1884-1932), the flamboyant reporter who gave his name to France's most prestigious journalism prize. "Our job," he famously said, "is not to please nor to displease, it is to put the pen in the wound."

He meant that journalists should be exclusively guided by the principle of truth, without fear or favour. When asked about his political line, the globe-trotting reporter responded: "I know only one line, the railway line."

In journalism, however, the lofty ideal of independence is often just that: an ideal. Complicity with one side of the story is constantly lurking in the background. Journalists instinctively wonder what reactions their reporting will provoke and what impact it will have on society and power but also, more selfishly, consider their status, their career, their sources and their friendships.

When, as a young journalist, I covered the Central American revolutions in the 1970s and 80s, my indignation at the brutality of the military *caudillos* was such that I was permanently torn. Should I really write that the Sandinista National Liberation Front (FSLN) was dogmatically Marxist and mentored by Cuban agents at the risk of undermining the broad

---

Sometimes newspapers made the choice on my behalf and spiked articles

opposition movement; or of condoning the rise to power of an authoritarian regime if I hid it? Sometimes newspapers made the choice on my behalf and spiked articles that did not fit the acceptable line. These dilemmas never abated as I grappled over the next few decades with stories – from the peace movement to the Iraq wars or terrorism – which bluntly raised the question of the consequences of my reporting or commentary on public opinion.

Complicity rhymes with conformity, and sometimes it relates to the prevalent cultural mood. It leads journalists to follow the dominant narrative and leave incovenient facts out of their stories. In the 1950s and 60s, the intellectual hegemony of Marxism was so powerful at Saint-Germain des Prés that, in left wing circles, "it was better to be wrong with Jean-Paul Sartre (the communist fellow traveller) than to be right with Raymond Aron (the lonesome Cold War liberal)". In the neoconservative 1980s it was mostly inconceivable for mainstream journalists to refer negatively to Afghan "freedom fighters" or to underline the presence within the Polish Solidarity movement of ultra-conservative figures such as the Kaczynski twins, as well as celebrated liberals such as Jacek Kuron or Bronislaw Geremek.

Today, as the new political hegemony has shifted rightwards in sync with the rise of national populism, liberal or left-leaning writers are shrinking from highlighting "negative stories" about refugees or Islam because they fear they will feed racism or be reprimanded by their progressive friends. On the "other side" the temptation to amplify those negative stories is too strong.

The eagerness to be anointed by prominent figures from one side or the other, as well as being in tune with the perceived public majority, inevitably feeds complicity and self-censorship. This comes at the cost of undermining the integrity of information that, according to Jürgen Habermas's theory in Truth in the Public Sphere, is essential to generate considered and reasonable public opinion.

Some in the French establishment media also practise a form of complicity which, if

→ less ideological, reflects a system of mutual benefit between journalism and power. French journalists' deference in front of their "elected monarch" has regularly been mocked by their Anglo-Saxon colleagues. In France, special access journalism, junkets and private presidential briefings are based on the assumption that the journalists who are the "chosen few" will be "on side" and complicit in the official narrative.

Often, complicity is driven by opportunism rather than by ideology. Without the support of state institutions, non-governmental organisations or corporations, some reporters would simply not be able to travel around the world. Their reluctance to be transparent about who sponsors their reportage testifies to the malaise.

Some invitations inevitably blur the lines between journalism and public relations and compromise the journalists' independence and integrity. Invited reporters who "spit in the soup" and dare to deviate from their hosts' narrative are few, and are expeditiously excommunicated.

Dealing with confidential sources can also lead to complicity. The leak that a source gives to a journalist may imply, as a quid pro quo, protection from critical coverage. The dilemmas of "revelation" journalism were bluntly and controversially addressed in a September 2019 essay in the leftist monthly Le Monde diplomatique by the late investigative journalist Pierre Péan. He implied, under the headline "Who benefits from the anticorruption struggle?", that a new generation of "investigators" were mainly puppets of the judicial and political authorities who leaked them stories, and accomplices in a drama that they did not control.

The risk of complicity underlines the need for diversity and pluralism in the media so that the silence of one on a specific issue will be compensated by the noise of the other

"Journalists pay for their access to (judicial) documents by an extreme dependence on their sources," he wrote. "When minutes of the proceedings come from the lawyers of the plaintiffs, the articles generally reflect the latter's point of view."

Journalism inevitably implies transactions and compromises. But complicity, whatever form it takes, is a scourge for journalism. It deprives the public of part of the facts that it needs to forge its "informed consent". When it is paired with conformity and the dominant narrative, it marginalises dissident voices who may be closer to the "truth", or may at least bring a minimum of balance in a story.

Jean-François Kahn, one of France's most famous maverick journalists, was particularly damning in an early January 2020 column in the Brussels daily Le Soir when he described how the French establishment press regularly crucified him when he begged to differ with Michel Foucault, Gilles Deleuze and other untouchables of the French intelligentsia.

Such perception of complicity also undermines journalists' credibility. According to the 2020 press barometer published by the Paris daily La Croix, only 25% of the French public think that journalists are independent from political parties or corporations.

The "complicity with the elites" is also behind the accusations and the physical agressions against the press by the *Gilets jaunes* (yellow vests) protesters who have turned media-bashing into a combat sport.

Finally, censoring "for a good cause" acts like a boomerang and destroys what it pretends to defend. Lately, under the pretext of fighting fascism or racism, well-meaning self-censors have provided the far right with the immense privilege of claiming that it is the only one "speaking the truth" and the opportunity of accusing the liberal or progressive media of belonging to the "lying press". In February, commenting on a controversy around blasphemy and the malaise it created in progressive circles, Jean Quatremer, the ebullient and influential Brussels correspondent of the liberal-left

French daily Liberation, did not mince his words: "Trapped by the Islamists' discourse on 'Islamophobia', part of Macron's party – and especially part of the left – has allowed the far right to hijack secularism (*laïcité*), freedom of expression, the right to atheism or feminism."

The risk of complicity underlines the need for diversity and pluralism in the media so that the silence of one on a specific issue will be compensated by the noise of the other.

But, much more fundamentally, it makes it imperative for journalists to assert their autonomy along the line of Walter Lippmann's adage in his 1920 essay, Liberty and the News:

"There can be no higher law in journalism than to tell the truth and shame the devil." ⊗

Jean-Paul Marthoz is a Belgian journalist who writes a column for Le Soir, and is on Index on Censorship's editorial board

Don't let them call the tune

Should we choose to speak at an event
sponsored by someone with whom we disagree?
Jeffrey Wasserstrom lays his thoughts
on the line

49(01): 14/16 I DOI: 10.1177/0306422020917595

ABOUT A DECADE ago, a China specialist
at a US university invited me to speak
on his campus, but he left out one important
detail. The sponsor of my talk would be the
local Confucius Institute.

Confucius Institutes are educational organisations, which are designed to promote goodwill
toward the People's Republic of China in other
countries. They get their funding from and are
supervised by the Hanban, which is part of the
Chinese Communist Party. And it was only
when I arrived and saw a poster advertising my
talk that I discovered the funding would come
from an organisation with ties to a government
whose record on human rights I deplore.

I realised then that I had a dilemma.

Would it be a form of complicity to go ahead
with the talk, knowing that the overall goal of
the Hanban is to encourage people around the
world to feel that the CCP is taking the country
in a positive direction?

I have always had deep misgivings about
Confucius Institutes, and I have been glad that
no institution with which I have been affiliated
has had one. It is true that they generally steer
clear of obvious political
messaging, but they often do
things which subtly reinforce
an official view of what
"China" is, and suggest that
Beijing has a monopoly over
what "Chineseness" means.

There have also been
suggestions that Confucius
Institutes discourage discussion of taboo topics, such
as the "Three Ts" of Tibet,
Tiananmen and Taiwan. I
have always dealt with those
three topics in my teaching in
a way that veers sharply from
the CCP official line.

Ever since I received my doctor-
ate – in the same spring when
troops killed large numbers of
unarmed protesters and bystanders
near Tiananmen Square – I have
been writing about the June 4th
Massacre, always referring to it
as a "massacre", and denouncing
the "Big Lie" promoted by Beijing
that the troops dealt with a "riot"
in a manner that showed restraint.

So, I asked myself when I saw
the poster, what options did I have?

At first, I thought there were
just two, and, given my convictions, really only one. I could refuse to speak and offer to eschew
reimbursement for my travel or
pay the university back. Or (and
this wasn't really an option in
my mind) I could go ahead as if
nothing had happened, giving
the talk I had planned – about
Shanghai as a global city – without engaging
with any particularly controversial subjects,
and then, afterwards, making clear that I
would have liked to have been told about
sponsorship in advance.

Fortunately, I realised that – as is often the
case with complicity and dissent – there were
not just two choices. I hit upon a third route.

I gave the talk I had planned, but prefaced

---

*It is important to ask oneself tough
questions about speaking out, or not,
and when and how and where to do so*

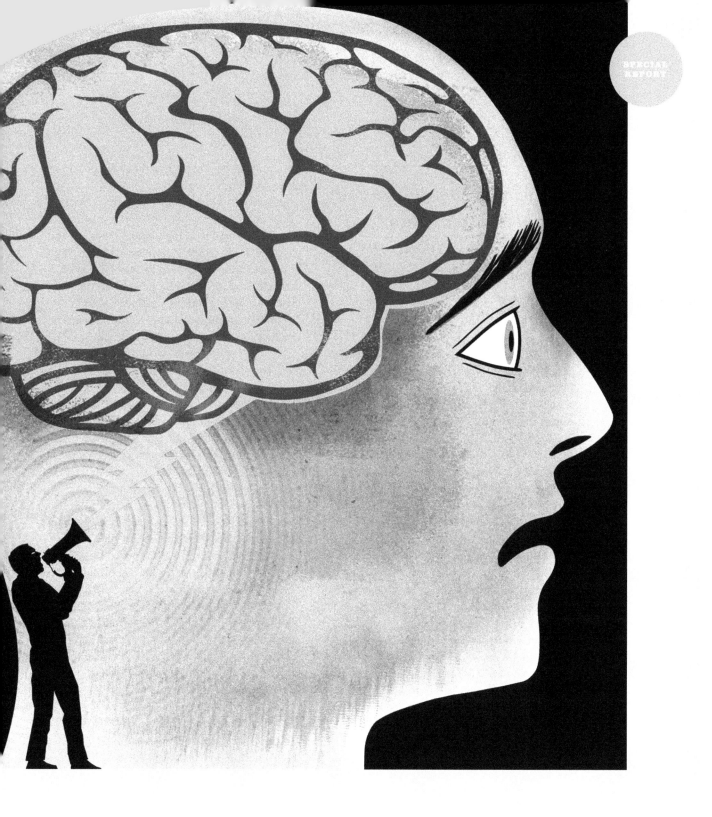

it with five minutes about Confucianism and the CCP, noting how ironic it was that the programme that brought me to campus was one tied to an organisation whose most famous leader, Mao Zedong, spearheaded campaigns to rid the country of all vestiges of "feudal" Confucian thought.

I also found ways to slip in comments that made clear my critical stance toward the CCP.

I began to adopt this improvised approach to all talks that were going to be sponsored or co-sponsored by a Confucius Institute.

A few years later, I got my first direct invitation from a Confucius Institute to speak.

I was uncomfortable with the invitation, but they said I could pick as controversial an approach to recent Chinese history and politics as I wanted.

She learned that the initially approved nomination had been blocked, due to my outspoken stance on the events of 1989

→ I decided to focus my talk on the ways that George Orwell's famous novel about Big Brother and Aldous Huxley's Brave New World both provided insights into the current situation in the PRC.

The talk went just fine, with lively questions, but I did wonder if there would be any ramifications when a report reached Beijing. I later learned that the write up on my talk had been either clueless or very clever: it said that I had given a talk about China and 1984, with language that made it seem that I might have been talking about a year in history, rather than a dystopian novel.

But not all has been rosy in my relationship with Confucius Institutes. A few years ago, a colleague at a US university told me she had nominated me to give the annual distinguished lecture on China.

Later, however, she learned that the initially approved nomination had been blocked, due to my outspoken stance on the events of 1989.

I have colleagues I respect who tell me that they have good working relationships with the Confucius Institutes on their campuses and do not feel any pressure to modify what they do.

I also have colleagues I respect who feel that giving a talk with even partial sponsorship from a Confucius Institute would feel like an unacceptable form of complicity with the CCP at a time when it is doing despicable things. I understand their position.

I speak out regularly about human-rights abuses, including the grotesque mistreatment of Uyghurs and members of other non-Han ethnic groups in Xinjiang. I also have been writing a lot about protests in Hong Kong, making it clear that, overall, the authorities have handled the situation abysmally and that the police have often used undue force.

People will occasionally tell me that behaving in this manner is "brave", since it could conceivably lead to being unable to get a visa to travel to the Chinese mainland or even, if things continue to develop as they have lately, get me banned from Hong Kong. I do not see myself as doing anything particularly gutsy or courageous, however, due to my personal circumstances and advanced career stage.

Having visa problems would not cut me off from friends or family members nor prevent me from completing work on a book I need to publish to get tenure. The risks of speaking out are so minimal that failing to do so would feel like complicity. I know people in my field I respect, though, who have more at stake and make different calculations.

There is also a notable case where I have stopped short of taking a vow related to human rights activity that many people I respect in my field have taken. I am thinking of the "Xinjiang Initiative", which was launched by some scholars of the PRC and called on signatories to "pledge to use every public event in which they appear to remind their audiences that roughly a million people are being held in extra-legal internment camps, and that these detentions are solely due to detainees' ethnicity or religion."

I did not take that pledge, even though I bring up the internment camps in nearly every public event I do. I was hesitant to sign on mostly because I could imagine a scenario in which bringing the topic up would have negative consequences for someone other than me.

Context matters. Seemingly black-and-white ideas about complicity often turn out, on closer inspection, to have grey areas. It is important to ask oneself tough questions about speaking out, or not, and when and how and where to do so. We go astray if we don't ask them, but we also go astray if we assume that they have easy or one-size-fits-all answers. ⊗

Jeffrey Wasserstrom is chancellor's professor of history at the University of California, Irvine

Chipping away at our privacy

As Swedes embrace a trend to have microchips implanted in their bodies, **Nathalie Rothschild** asks if this is the ultimate privacy invasion

49(01): 17/19 I DOI: 10.1177/0306422020917596

IT'S A GREY, chilly day in March, and a handful of self-described techies have gathered at an unassuming basement office in an upscale part of central Stockholm for a "chipping" event.

They are getting glass-encased microchips implanted between their thumbs and index fingers – the incision is quick but stings and feels a bit like being stabbed with a fork, says 19-year-old student Olof.

"I wanted one because it's cool and it's something us techies are into because we like being at the forefront of technological developments," he explained.

Radio-frequency identification microchips use the same technology found in credit cards, key fobs and public transport passes. In Sweden, companies ranging from the national rail service to a water park have installed such readers, meaning that anyone who has been chipped can, with a simple swipe of the hand, open doors, pay at vending machines or validate tickets.

Sina Amoor Pour, a bio-engineer trained to perform chip implants, lets the chipping event attendees into the building by swiping his hand against a reader. Amoor Pour says that today's crowd is pretty typical: males across a fairly wide age range.

Olof plans to copy his public transport pass to his new chip. By cloning the travel pass, Olof can ditch his plastic card.

Implanted microchips, enthusiasts like to emphasise, replace the need to carry around passes, keys and credit cards. But you can't use a single microchip at multiple locations, which is why a few of the attendees at the Stockholm chipping event are opting for two implants.

"I'll use the one in my right hand for the underground and the one in my left hand at the gym," said 24-year-old Adam.

The RFID chips are passive, meaning they don't have a battery or power source, and so do nothing until they interact with a reader. Since they don't emit a signal, they can't be tracked. But there are microchips that use near-field communication and these can store data, such as your contact details and blood type. Some choose to add virtual business cards to their implants, which can be shared using a smartphone app.

It's that ability to store data that causes some to fear they make bearers vulnerable to hacking. Although you cannot currently store a large amount of data on the microchips, they may become more sophisticated in the future and, even today, if you have an NFC reader on your phone and place it against someone's chip you can read the information off it. With an NFC reader/writer, you can also change a chip's content.

"The more data is stored in a single space, the more attractive the chips will be to hackers," said Ben Libberton, a science communicator based in Stockholm.

"You have to consider the issue of keeping the gathered data safe, as well as the question of how the data is harnessed." He believes there should be safeguards in place and that lawmakers should regulate the microchips.

Back at the chipping event in Stockholm, Adam says he thinks there's little need to →

Biohackers are driven by distrust, or at least by a desire to wrest their own personal data away from third parties

CHIPS WITH EVERYTHING

IIIIIIIIIIIIIIIIIIIIIIIIIIIIIIIIIIIIIIIIIIIIIIIIIIII

Orna Herr takes a look at the companies using microchips to keep tabs on us

NEW JEANS? NEW TRACKING DEVICE
Tommy Hilfiger added Tommy Jeans Xplore to its range in 2018, a clothing line in which each item has a Bluetooth smart-chip installed. The chip is linked to an app which allows the company to track how often the customer is wearing the clothes and where.

ALEXA IS LISTENING
Reports have emerged that Amazon staff listen to recordings in order to "improve the customer experience" of that small, voice-activated device in the corner of the room. Internal chat rooms exist for staff to swap funny things they hear and distressing activities.

BIG BROTHER, BIG BOSS
Crossover, a talent management company, was said to be using surveillance technology that included taking photos of employees at their desks every 10 minutes. Tracking devices have also been used on nurses in a hospital in Florida, USA, to help the hospital know which stations need a bigger stock of medical supplies.

→ worry about hacking or privacy breaches. "The implants aren't visible and I'm not a public figure. You'd have to know that I was wearing a microchip and then get up pretty close to scan my hand with a reader. Why would someone go through all that trouble? After all, you can find lots of personal data, including my home address, through a simple internet search. I'm also walking around at all times with a device that is truly traceable – my smartphone."

The organisers of the chipping event are "biohackers" – DIY biological engineers who often experiment on their own bodies. Biohackers are the pioneers of the microchipping trend, which by some estimates has been adopted by around 4,000 Swedes as well as others around the world. But the biohacking scene in Sweden is different from scenes elsewhere, says Moa Petersén, a lecturer in digital cultures at the University of Lund.

"Biohacking movements vary in character, and the way it's developed in a particular country to some extent reflects the local society and culture," said Petersén, whose book The Swedish Microchipping Phenomenon came out last year.

What's notable about how it has developed in Sweden is that it is celebrated and done in the open, with companies organising implant parties as PR stunts and as an activity at staff events.

At a 2017 seminar organised by the national rail company, Karin Svensson Smith – who was then a member of the government's transport commission – got microchipped in front of a press scrum and told reporters it would make travelling by train a "more seamless" experience.

"Microchipping has been de-dramatised here in Sweden," said Petersén. For her, the Swedes' overall tech-positive attitude, along with a high level of trust and the safety net offered by the welfare state, comprise the trinity that holds the key to understanding why the trend has taken a relatively strong hold in Sweden.

She says that the biohackers she interviewed wanted to "take control of their own data".

At present, the microchips do little more than act as digital badges, even if many evangelists believe the future of implant tech lies in more advanced usage. Among those evangelists is Hannes Sapiens, a pioneer of the trend, who has travelled around the world to give talks about implant tech.

"Sweden is a high-trust society and that has certainly been a factor," he said. "However, it's my conviction that the most important factor for implant tech taking off here is that Sweden is a powerfully tech-literate society… and if you understand how a technology works, you also understand that you need not be afraid of it as long as you use it in the right way."

Sapiens is not overly concerned about the risk of privacy infringement and says chip implants cannot be used for surveillance purposes "in any meaningful way".

He lists three reasons. First, the RFID chips are passive – they can't be tracked since they

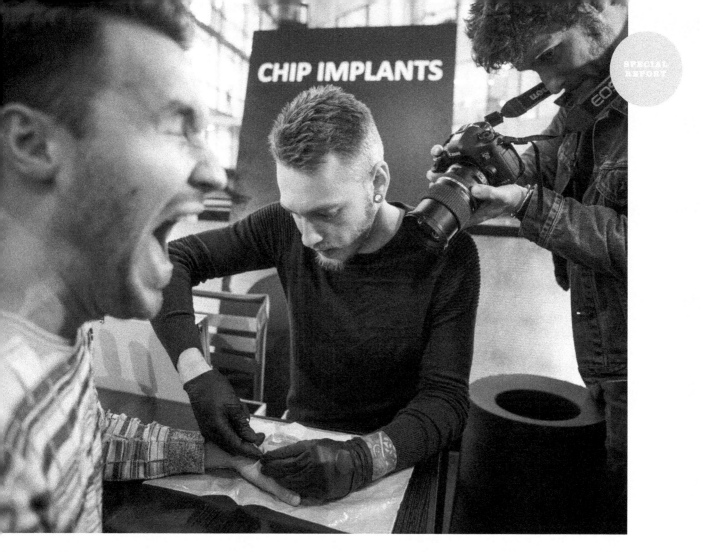

CHIP IMPLANTS

don't emit signals. Second, in order to activate the chip implant you have to touch it to a reader; and while someone can scan it without your consent, they would have to get up close since the chips can't be read at a distance. Third, the implants can't collect data. They are repositories of data that you have to actively put into them.

Sapiens also believes the chips are a more privacy-friendly alternative to biometric identification technologies such as face recognition and fingerprints.

It's that possibility to control and protect one's data that drives microchip enthusiasts. Arguably, biohackers are driven by distrust, or at least by a desire to wrest their own personal data away from third parties. Jowan Österlund, founding CEO of Biohax International, says he has microchipped about 6,000 people around the world, the majority of them in Sweden. He himself has four microchip implants.

"The coolest thing about it is that it allows me to lock my digital identity. That means I own and control my digital identity," he said.

Despite his reservations, Libberton believes implants offer "huge potential" for monitoring health. "All things being equal, I would love to have that kind information myself. The question is – and this is my main reservation – how do I get that information? Does it come straight to me, and is it private? Or is it shared with other companies so that, if my glucose levels increase, I can suddenly get an increase in my health-insurance premiums?"

Libberton does not have a principled objection to integrating technology into the body but he is concerned about how the information is gathered and shared.

"My main worry is that we're becoming more and more willing to sacrifice privacy for the sake of convenience." ⊗

Nathalie Rothschild is a journalist based in Stockholm

ABOVE: A man has a microchip inserted under his skin at a "chipping" event at Epicenter, Stockholm in 2018. Some estimates put the number of Swedes who have been chipped at 4,000

There's nothing wrong with being scared

Reporter **Kirsten Han** used to think older journalists were weak for not covering a controversial story, but now she's starting to understand why

49(01): 20/21 I DOI: 10.1177/0306422020917599

SINGAPORE'S GOVERNMENT IS debating the introduction of yet more legislation.

This time, it says it's going after "foreign interference" – which will be defined however the ruling People's Action Party would like it to be.

Last September, my organisation and I were namechecked in a speech by K Shanmugam, minister for home affairs and law, about the potential legislation, so I have every expectation of being adversely affected by its inevitable passage.

For months, I've wondered ahead of every sitting of parliament if this is going to be the one at which an anti-foreign interference bill will be tabled. I'm still waiting.

Since the Protection from Online Falsehoods and Manipulation Act – a law giving the government extremely broad powers, ostensibly to combat "fake news" – came into effect in October last year, I've found myself hesitating over my work in ways more pronounced than ever before.

I dawdle over things that I would have simply proceeded with previously. I second-guess interviews I've done. I run through every paranoid scenario in my mind, highly conscious that I'm operating in an environment where the government would seize any opportunity to discredit prominent critical voices or shut down dissent. I feel like the margin of error that I'm allowed is zero. I wonder how feasible that is in a context where there is no freedom of information and no whistleblower protection, and where investigative journalism barely exists.

I have started dragging my heels on some stories. I tell myself that I'm busy with other things but, in reality, I know I'm afraid. Not of penalties such as fines or jail time – although they'd certainly be unpleasant – but of the mental and emotional burden.

I know what I can expect because I've been through some of it before: the online trolling from the pro-ruling party camp, the smug viral posts spreading misinformation about me on social media, the misogynist comments on forum pages, the newspaper articles that trigger anxiety among my closest family members, the sense of being marked, the uncertainty of whether things might escalate further, and what else I might have to face.

It's draining to think of these potential consequences. It feels as if it would be easier simply not to approach that line, not to attract that sort of trouble. So stories get postponed indefinitely, and self-censorship digs in a little deeper.

This is a position I'd naively imagined I would always be able to avoid. As a young journalist, I had viewed the mainstream media journalists who'd reported on the use of detention without trial in 1987 with contempt. In that year, the government rounded up 22 volunteers, social workers and theatre practitioners, accused them of a "Marxist conspiracy" to overthrow Singapore's elected government, and threw them behind bars. No evidence was ever presented before a judge, and no one was convicted in a court of law.

The main newspaper published ministry statements verbatim, while televised confessions

---

I have started dragging my heels on some stories. I tell myself that I'm busy with other things

CREDIT: Bridgeman Images/Diane Ong

– which the former detainees say were made under duress – were recorded and broadcast. When I first learnt about this period of history, I saw the journalists and editors of these media outlets as complicit in the oppression and the state-led smear campaign, surrendering their professional integrity to play ball.

Years later, when working as a stringer for a wire agency filing breaking news from Singapore, I found myself typing up ministry statements about how they'd detained individuals under the very same law used in 1987. This time, the government claimed that the individuals had been detained because they'd been radicalised into supporting Isis, and needed to be taken into custody as part of Singapore's counter-terrorism efforts.

Apart from that government statement there was no other source. There was no way to get access to the accused individuals to interview them and I was highly unlikely to find anyone who knew those people to give on-the-record comments. The police weren't going to say anything that different from the Ministry of Home Affairs, and there was no chance that showing up at the detention centre would yield any result. Yet journalists for other outlets were certainly filing stories, and if their pieces came out without a peep from me, my editors would be demanding answers.

I filed the story.

Democracies operate via leaders elected by the will of the people, but authoritarian political systems also require the co-operation of their citizens. Often all that's needed is a decision to look the other way or not push back.

It might not stem from malicious intent or some craven desire to suck up to power. But

There was no way to get access to the accused individuals to interview them and I was highly unlikely to find anyone who knew those people to give on-the-record comments

non-resistance is complicity all the same.

When we allow ourselves to give in to oppression and to self-censor, we become complicit in the system, taking on the burden of policing ourselves in ways that ultimately suit authoritarian and oppressive institutions. We might not be doing this willingly, but the ultimate effect of a disempowered, "obedient" population is achieved anyway.

Fighting self-censorship and self-policing isn't easy. It gets especially tricky when such patterns of behaviour become entrenched and normalised.

There's nothing wrong with being scared or hesitant, especially when the situation gives us reason to be. It's also unrealistic to expect moral purity and imagine that any of us can live without being complicit in any problematic or oppressive structures.

We might not be expected to lead revolutions, but more often than not it is the act of staying still that's the true complicity. And we can't be constantly letting ourselves off the hook. ⊗

Kirsten Han is editor-in-chief of south-east Asian democracy movement New Naratif. She writes frequently on social justice, human rights, politics and democracy

How to ruin a good dinner party

Jemimah Steinfeld asks why some topics are off the menu when it comes to polite conversation

49(01): 22/23 | DOI: 10.1177/0306422020917602

IT STARTED WHEN I was a child. My parents told me not to let the religious – and specifically the religious Jewish person – know that I ate non-kosher food. "It might make them feel awkward," they said. So, I kept quiet, eating my *treif* (non-kosher food) elsewhere. If we went out for Chinese meals, which happened often in my household, we had to keep this information hidden from our relatives because: "What would they think?" One memorable occasion was when we ran into the brother of a very religious friend tucking into pork spareribs. We all gave each other a knowing look that said "never speak of this again".

If only it began and ended with food on the table.

Over the years I have learnt there are topics that you only discuss and challenge if you feel really strongly about them. Circumcision, for example. Speak out against it and you could soon find yourself ostracised. I was relieved when, recently, I had a child four days after a friend's son was born. It gave me a ready-made excuse to not attend the *bris* (circumcision party) without saying why I was actually not attending. We're still friends; she has no idea.

But no single topic is likely to send you to a blacklist quicker than saying the "wrong" thing about Israel. This has, sadly, become a lot worse recently. As Israel's government has swung to the right, so have some in the Jewish community. And because these people are often

the oldest or the loudest, their voices are the ones that have dominated. I have become used to discussing the subject only with those I vet as ultra-left-wing, or not Jewish at all. Those I know would share similar values. There are, after all, plenty of other topics to talk about, so why bring up the ones I know will create friction? Why ruin a good dinner party? In short, I have housed myself in my own echo chamber.

The biggest flashpoint in my life, though, was the December 2019 general election in the UK, when the conversation turned to whether Labour leader Jeremy Corbyn was an anti-Semite (and headed a party of anti-Semites). In Jewish circles, the jury had made its decision – he most definitely was. Say anything contrary to that and you would be labelled a rabid anti-Semite yourself.

In this arena there was only one side – forget about debate, nuance, reason, even agreeing to disagree. I pondered writing about my feelings (namely that while some claims of anti-Semitism stood up, I wasn't convinced by all). Some brave souls did speak out. The author Michael Rosen, for example, was very vocal about the fact he felt the charge of anti-Semitism was being weaponised for political gain. Rosen – with his 162,000 followers, his multi-million-pound book empire, his age, his maleness – had the guts where I, and others in my community, did not.

Instead I watched, quiet, at the sidelines as my Facebook feed became a bulletin board of people declaring that we needed to vote in a certain way if we wanted to avoid the Fourth Reich. People spoke for me, as a British Jew, even though I didn't share their views. I made one attempt to discuss this topic over dinner with relatives, during which I was likened to the disillusioned Jews in Weimar Germany who thought Hitler could be contained. Needless to say, I made no further attempts. The family decided politics was off the menu for meals after that.

I was not the only one having such heated conversations. As reported in the New York Times: "Online and over Shabbat dinners, arguments about the election have grown bitter. Those grudgingly planning to vote for Labour have been called traitors to the community and self-hating Jews."

The election has been and gone, but it's left a nasty aftertaste. And the paramount question: What topic will become the next conversational minefield? US President Donald Trump's Middle East peace plan?

As a British Jew whose family was murdered in the Holocaust, I champion the protection of minority rights. Indeed, I work day-in, day-out to promote these. I believe we need to practise religious tolerance, that we need to make everyone feel welcome whatever their faith, and that we need to keep calling out anti-Semitism until this religious hatred is relegated to history textbooks. What I do not believe in is the shutting down of entirely reasonable discussions, nor in bold claims escaping forensic examination, nor in granting some views more respect than others just because those espousing them might offend more easily.

Have I contributed to this censorial environment? In a way, yes. Every time I have kept shtum, I have helped foster an atmosphere where only one opinion is valid. My people-pleasing, my desire to not ruin a nice dinner, to maintain friends on Facebook and good relationships with relatives – all of this has had the unintended effect of emboldening some people, of silencing the views of others, and of making people less confident – on all sides – in dealing with confrontation. We don't need more confrontation in this world, but we do need to know how to deal with it when it emerges.

Of course, this extends beyond Jewish circles: my non-believer friends who have Christenings so as not to offend grandparents; the people who shrug off racist jokes from elderly uncles – many trade free expression for an easy life.

There is a reason German Lutheran pastor Martin Niemöller's poem First They Came is so often quoted – because people recognise their own shortcomings in its words. Democracy dies not in grand gestures but in the moments when we are weak and complicit. When we don't speak up when we know we could, or when we feel we should. I have bitten my tongue for too long; I hope that I won't continue. But I can't

I attempted to discuss Labour's anti-Semitism over dinner with relatives... I was likened to the disillusioned Jews in Weimar Germany

promise that. The wine might be flowing, the food delicious, and so when that older, more conservative guest starts spouting off unpalatable views I might just bring up The Masked Singer instead.

Jemimah Steinfeld is deputy editor at Index on Censorship

Sshh... no speaking out

Alison Flood spoke to Tom Holland, Mary Fulbrook, Serhii Plokhy and Daniel Beer about when, and where, the public has agreed to be silenced

49(01): 24/27 | DOI: 10.1177/0306422020917605

"**WE KNOW, OF** course, there's really no such thing as the 'voiceless'," said Arundhati Roy, in a lecture after winning the Sydney Peace Prize in 2004. "There are only the deliberately silenced or the preferably unheard."

But what about those who choose to be silenced, to give away their right to free speech because it means they will be safer, or richer, or given better jobs – or even that they can simply stay alive? We spoke to four historians to explore situations when people have agreed to be silenced, and the consequences this can have.

For the award-winning historian Tom Holland, the "primal" example of this in the west is the Roman empire. Initially a republic founded on the ideal of freedom of speech, Rome became an autocracy, and its people stopped having the right to say what they wanted.

"The emblematic symbol of the end of the republic is the murder [in 43BC] of Cicero, who was the greatest orator in Rome,

RIGHT: (top to bottom) Historians Tom Holland, Mary Fulbrook, Serhii Plokhy and Daniel Beer

a man who was naturally inclined to a mingled arrogance and timidity," he said. "After Caesar's assassination, Cicero stands up and is counted and attempts to stand firm against what he sees as the reintroduction of tyranny by Caesar's followers, particularly Mark Antony, and then, in due course, Julius Caesar's adopted son, who will end up becoming Augustus."

When Mark Antony and his triumvirate agree to murder those who have opposed them, Cicero is cornered and killed, his hands nailed to the rostra in the forum. "His head is delivered to Mark Antony's wife, and she pulls the tongue out and stabs it with her hairpins. So you have both the tongue and the hands being symbolically abused. And this becomes an emblematic symbol," said Holland.

The poet Ovid is then exiled, which "has a chilling effect on subsequent generations".

"[They] make a choice not to speak out and you don't really have someone like an Ovid again," Holland added. "Under Nero you have Lucan and you have Petronius, both of whom are great writers and both of whom end up committing forced suicide. So there's a definite sense that every time any writer in Rome seems to be given any slack under the emperors, if they go too far, then you know that then it's curtains for them."

Holland highlights Tacitus, who he feels is the writer who "reflects on this with the greatest sense of guilt".

"Tacitus is a senator, well-born, has provincial commands [and] serves within the framework of the Roman state under Domitian, who is another terrifyingly tyrannical emperor. Under Domitian he's essentially kept quiet, kept his head down, taken the rewards. Tacitus has a political career, so in that sense he collaborates. He keeps his head down, but he also collaborates. And he's aware of that," he said.

After Domitian's assassination in 96AD, Tacitus went on to write his great works, the

Often these denunciations took place at meetings, in front of hundreds of people sitting in the aisles

Histories and the Annals. "Tacitus portrays [earlier emperor] Tiberius's reign as one in which the shadows darken and darken, and lengthen and lengthen. He traces the way in which, slowly, people are brought to compromise themselves. It's a brilliant and timeless anatomy of how that process happens. And because it's Rome, and Rome stands at the wellspring of the western political tradition, it's had a huge, huge influence on the way that people in subsequent generations and periods of crisis have seen it; on the way that people thought about Stalinism and fascism."

Mary Fulbrook, whose Reckonings: Legacies of Nazi Persecution and the Quest for Justice won the 2019 Wolfson History Prize, highlights the silencing of the poor, uneducated classes who were called up to Germany's Reich Labour Service in 1940 and '41. "They found themselves being sent to work at the sanatoria for the mentally and physically disabled that were being used as euthanasia institutes," she said. "They had to pledge in advance that they would keep completely silent about what it was they were going to do in advance of being sent there, [without] knowing what they were going to do. They'd get there, they'd find themselves being care assistants, helping undress people who were about to be gassed.

"The Reich Labour Service would say: 'there are a couple of jobs available, a pretty lousy job in a factory, and a rather better one in a sanatorium in south-west Germany, how do you fancy it? But you have to sign this pledge

LEFT AND FAR LEFT: The assassination of Caesar led by Brutus and Cassius

ABOVE: Members of the Reich Labour Service march at the Nuremburg Rally, 1934

In one "particularly vile" case, says Fulbrook, a doctor successfully argued in the West German courts "that he had 'only killed 90 children' in order to keep his job and prevent somebody worse taking his job, who would have killed all 180 he was supposed to kill".

"The silencing of the very low-level care assistants, the ordinary workers, was subsequently misused as evidence of their knowledge of wrongdoing," she said. "Whereas at the time, I think it was evidence of their total powerlessness, and being offered a rubbish job or a better job, on the basis that they kept quiet about what the job entails."

Russia specialist Daniel Beer, whose The House of the Dead: Siberian Exile Under the Tsars won the 2017 Cundill History Prize, highlights a similar period, albeit a very different situation.

"In the 1930s, in the Soviet Union, during what's become known as the Great Terror, people could be accused of being enemies of the state on the most spurious of grounds, just denounced by rivals in the workplace. Often, these denunciations took place at meetings, in front of hundreds of people sitting in the aisles. Someone would stand up, a denunciation would be made, and then the assembled people would be invited to speak in favour of either the prosecution or the defence," said Beer.

"There are countless examples where people were understandably terrified to raise their voices in defence of those they knew to be to innocent because they were concerned that they themselves would be singled out next. People who quietly toed the line because if you want job security, if you want promotion, if you

→ to keep silent about what it is you will see and do.' So, the silence could advance, not knowing what it is they're going to be silenced about. They then go and discover what it is they're involved in."

One young woman, named as Erna Sch, Fulbrook says, was "so shocked and horrified and upset to be the 'care assistant' to people about to be gassed" that "she really couldn't bear it and wanted to leave". She wasn't allowed to. She got herself pregnant twice, in the hope that two successive maternity leaves and two small children might stop her employment, but she still couldn't escape it.

"And after the war, she was sentenced to three years' imprisonment by an East German court," said Fulbrook. "One of the arguments made in the post-war German courts was that if you signed a pledge of silence you knew that what you were about to do must be criminal, illegal, immoral, wrong in some way. So, the pledge to remain silent was used in post-war courts as proof of knowledge of wrongdoing for these very low-level people, who got given sentences of two to three years in prison, while those who were actually doing the stuff – the doctors, the people who were higher up in the hierarchy – usually managed to wangle their way out of these cases."

FAR LEFT: German women who have been drafted into the Reich Labour Service, on their way to an agricultural posting, 1938

LEFT: Men at work in the nuclear power plant in Chernobyl where there was a massive nuclear accident in 1986

want your own research institute to be looked upon favourably by the authorities, you just keep your head down, you don't say things that anger those in power."

There is a "sliding scale" here, says Beer, from times when it "really was a matter of life and death", to more latterly, "when you weren't going to be pulled off to the firing squad or the gulags, but you might find your promotion at work blocked, or find it very difficult to get your journalism or your fiction published".

"People in those positions just sort of quietly kept their heads down and toed the line, rather than taking positions that would bring them into political dissent," he said.

"One of the mechanisms clearly at work in Russia in the 20th century was also self-censorship. People don't sit there and think: 'I am now making a pointless decision to suppress the truth.' They are so personally and professionally and ideologically invested in the success of a particular kind of project, they find themselves inflating their successes and glossing over failures and shortcomings because they don't want to bring the system into disrepute."

And this sort of censorship, or self-censorship, continued well into the 1970s and 1980s. "There is this long afterlife of Stalinism. One of the sources of the regime's power is that if you visit such horrendous violence on your own population, as the Soviet state did in the 1930s and 1940s, you have then traumatised generations. Even though, objectively, the

threat is maybe not of the same magnitude, they are so habituated to the requirements of not speaking out, keeping your head down, that it becomes almost embedded in the cultural DNA and survives long after the regime has loosened up again [and] is no longer as terroristic as it used to be," said Beer.

Serhii Plokhy, whose history of Chernobyl won the 2018 Baillie Gifford Prize, points to a similar dovetailing of censorship and self-censorship for those working in nuclear energy facilities in the Soviet Union.

"People were involved during the Cold War in all sorts of nuclear projects, and most of them – at least originally – were linked to the bomb. That culture, at least in the Soviet Union, was then transferred to the nuclear energy facilities, which were not involved with the bomb anymore, but the technology was still considered to be secret," he said. "And these people were signing all sorts of papers saying that they would not talk about what they have seen or what they experience – they wouldn't talk to their partners, to their children, to their neighbours."

The reward was that you kept your job; the threat was that if you did speak out, you could end up in a gulag. "People were keeping silent partially because they believed they had no other choice. They were obliged, according to whatever regulations and laws were in place," he said. "But also, some of them truly believed that, as patriotic citizens, they couldn't [speak publicly] because the enemy could get all sorts of important information. Our secrets are our secrets. That was very much in the air at the time." ⊗

Alison Flood is a freelance journalist who specialises in literary news and is a regular contributor to Index on Censorship

Making foes out of friends

Steven Borowiec talks to a North Korean defector who is protesting the South Korean government's unwillingness to tackle the North's human rights record during current political negotiations

49(01): 28/30 I DOI: 10.1177/0306422020917607

KIM TAE-HEE BEDS down each night on the same patch of pavement where, a few months ago, she collapsed while on the brink of starvation.

She is maintaining a round-the-clock sit-in in the busiest part of the South Korean capital, in front of the Ministry of Unification – South Korea's government agency that handles relations with North Korea – to draw attention to what she sees as an emergency: the dire circumstances faced by many North Korean defectors who live in the South.

Her presence here started when she and a few other activists embarked on hunger strikes to call on the government to investigate two troubling, high-profile incidents involving North Koreans. In late December, after 12 days without eating, Kim lost consciousness and was rushed to hospital.

While shaken by that experience, she is continuing her campaign, albeit with regular eating habits. On this particular chilly winter

The left, currently in power, contends that drawing attention to abuses in the North will scare North Korea away from the negotiating table

night, Kim is huddled on a heated groundsheet with three guests – a fellow North Korean activist, a South Korean pastor and a journalist – who are sharing North Korean-style rice cakes, glutinous blobs of rice flour coated in sweetener.

"This government refuses to acknowledge that North Korea is a failed society and they want to suppress anyone who points that out," Kim told Index from inside the tent.

"President Moon Jae-in and his government are ignoring North Korea's grave human rights abuses in a misguided effort to mollify [North Korean President] Kim Jong-un and improve relations with Pyongyang, but by doing so, they betray the long-suffering people of North Korea," said Phil Robertson, Asia deputy director at Human Rights Watch.

Since taking power in 2017, the government of President Moon Jae-in has carried out unprecedented shows of rapprochement with North Korea, starting with the North's participation in the 2018 Winter Olympics in the South, and including summits between leaders.

Kim and other critics argue that to accomplish these headline-grabbing feats, Moon has made a Faustian agreement to never mention the dire human rights abuses in the North, while working to depict North Korea as a normal country with a leadership that sincerely plans to get rid of its nuclear weapons.

After three inter-Korean summits, co-operation between the two sides is currently frozen and the Moon administration has no tangible achievements it can point to as evidence of the efficacy of this approach. The lack of progress with North Korea is one factor working against Moon as his administration faces crucial general elections in April.

While sleeping in a tent on a pavement through the winter may be a daunting prospect for most, Kim can handle it. Kim, 48, fled North Korea, one of the world's most repressive societies, in 1997 for China. Over the next 10 years, as she attempted to save enough money to get to South Korea, she was arrested three times by police and sent back to the

North. Each time she fled again, and eventually she made it to Seoul in 2007.

She admits that in the South she has found freedom and opportunities that never would have been available to her in the North, but two events in recent months have shaken her faith in her adopted homeland, and driven her to take action. In September last year, South Korea's defector community was shocked when the bodies of Han Sung-ok, 42, and her six-year-old son were found in a low-rent apartment in Seoul, apparently after having starved to death.

The headlines wrote themselves: a person who fled a poor country ended up starving to death in a rich country. Kim said she and other defectors wondered how the mother and son were left to die slowly without intervention

from the authorities. South Korea's Child Welfare Act mandates local governments to step in and provide the necessities of life to a child if a parent is unable or unwilling to.

Another incident occurred a few months later when the South Korean government announced that it had repatriated two North Korean fishermen who were accused of murdering 16 fellow crew members and dumping their bodies into the waters west of South Korea. Under South Korean law, all North Koreans are entitled to South Korean citizenship and must be allowed to remain in the South if they choose. The Seoul government sent the fishermen back to the North even though they asked to remain.

Kim would like the South Korean government to consult her and others with

The headlines wrote themselves: a person who fled a poor country ended up starving to death in a rich country

→ experience living in North Korea, a country that practises capital punishment and maintains a large, brutal network of prison camps.

The case involving the fishermen was particularly concerning for defectors and people still in North Korea. "That made people think that South Korea is a country where the government doesn't follow its own laws. People looked at those young men being sent back, and they saw how they were treated and wondered, 'Could that happen to me?' Or to their son or their brother," Kim said.

"The Moon government talks about peace and co-operation, but they refuse to even discuss how the policies of the North Korean government affect the people who live there. Everything they do goes through the regime and does nothing to help the people of North Korea."

Kim sees her role as helping South Koreans understand what North Korea is really like. "I can still see with the eyes of a North Korean," she said.

Explaining the repatriation, Lee Sang-min, a spokesman for the Ministry of Unification, told reporters that the two North Koreans had committed murder and were therefore not eligible for protection under South Korean law.

"We consulted among various government bodies and made the decision out of consideration of the South Korean people's safety," Lee said at a press conference.

More generally, in explaining its tendency to avoid speaking out about North Korea, the Moon administration has pointed to Article 4 of the South Korean constitution, which states that "the Republic of Korea shall seek unification and shall formulate and carry out a policy of peaceful unification".

Whether or not to press North Korea on its rights record is an old source of disagreement between the right and left of South Korea's political spectrum. The right argues that the suffering in the North is intolerable and that keeping silent about abuses serves only to legitimise a dictatorship and undermine South Korea's reputation as a state that respects human rights. The left, currently in power, contends that drawing attention to abuses in the North will scare North Korea away from the negotiating table. Overt condemnations of North Korean human rights abuses will thwart progress before it starts, the thinking goes, making it prudent to refrain from finger-wagging.

It is not only domestic groups that have been critical of Moon. In December 2019, 67 international human rights groups sent him an open letter criticising the repatriation of the fishermen, and the government's decision not to co-sponsor a UN resolution on North Korean human rights.

Another veteran activist, Doh Hee-youn, 52, argues that the Moon administration's North Korea policy is one reason behind the number of North Koreans defecting to South Korea in 2019 being the lowest in 18 years.

"Even while sanctions are creating ever harsher conditions there, people in the North no longer look at South Korea as a place where they can feel safe, and some therefore think it's better to stay put for now," Doh said in an interview at his office in Seoul.

Doh is best known as the activist who worked to smuggle the manuscript of The Accusation, a novel by Bandi, a pseudonymous writer in North Korea, out of the country.

He still has contacts in the North and says that, with the country subject to harsh international sanctions and rapprochement with the South going nowhere, times are tense. "People are increasingly dissatisfied," Doh said. "The tension is building up. Eventually, it will explode." ⊗

Steven Borowiec *is a freelance writer based in Seoul, South Korea*

Nothing in life is free

Are we choosing to give away our privacy to get free apps and services and what are the consequences? **Mark Frary** investigates

49(01): 31/33 I DOI: 10.1177/0306422020917608

SOME OF THE most useful parts of the internet are free. Take Google Maps: this year, on its 15th birthday, the company revealed that it was now used by more than one billion people around the globe. But what does free actually mean?

I am usually logged in to my Google account when I use Google Maps. Logging in makes the online experience seamless, particularly when you are using more than one device. It remembers websites you have visited and passwords between browsers, for example. On Google Maps you can define places such as your home or office, making it easy to calculate commute times and driving directions for regularly visited places. It also offers recommendations on places to eat and more.

But just take a look at your timeline (it's in the "hamburger" menu). Mine shows more than 700 places which I have visited in the past six years.

Google's argument for retaining this would be that it uses your location to provide everyday services and, naturally, locally relevant adverts. It is, after all, in the business of making money.

But what if your government is also interested in where you have been? Perhaps you visited the offices of the opposition several times last year.

For Google to give a government access to your data, that government has to make the request in writing. It must be signed by an authorised official and the request must be made in response to a legal process under an appropriate law.

That sounds like an onerous process, but it did not stop more than 75,000 such requests for user data – not including user account details – in the first half of 2019, according to a Google transparency report. The number of requests has more than doubled in four years. Should individuals be worried? Well, in the last set of figures available Google says it revealed user data in answer to 73% of those requests.

You don't have to accept this. You can turn off the location services on your device, or for specific applications, and you can delete this location history.

In 2019, the company finally added the incognito mode to Maps, which allows you to search and get directions without that information being saved to your Google account.

However, the vast majority of people choose not to use it, although some actively do so to use these free services.

The reality is that free services are not free, and many of those billions of users are happy to be complicit in order to make their lives easier.

A 2019 survey by the Centre for Data Innovation looked at the trade-off between exchanging data and access to online services. It found that 80% of users in the USA wanted Facebook and Google to collect less of their data. However, when asked what trade-offs they would make in order for this to happen they became more ambivalent. When asked if they would accept less data collection but lose some of the functionality of these services, support fell to 64%. When asked if they would pay a monthly subscription fee in order for Facebook and Google to collect less of their data, support dropped to just 25%.

Some of the platforms have considered this idea. Speaking in 2018, Facebook COO Sheryl Sandberg told NBC that while the company

---

Privacy should be a right, not a privilege, and not part of a Faustian bargain

WEB PRIVACY...

already had different forms of opt-out for users wanting to protect their data, there was currently no way to opt out of everything. "We don't have an opt-out at the highest level," she said. "That would be a paid product."

This idea has become known as "pay for privacy" – those who choose not to hand over personal information will be charged more or will receive a second-class experience.

"Privacy should be a right, not a privilege, and not part of a Faustian bargain," said Bennett Cyphers, staff technologist at the Electronic Frontier Foundation.

He believes that Google and others "coerce or require users to agree to absurd amounts of data sharing in order to sign up". He said: "Most of the data they collect is not necessary to provide the services they offer and is instead used to profile and monetise users through ads."

"The default should always be that Google doesn't collect such sensitive data unless you specifically ask it to, and that it doesn't use that data for anything you don't want."

Phil Barden, who runs the marketing agency Decode, said: "We want to use TikTok or Snapchat because there is a social motivation to do so because all your friends are on it and we want to use it now. This is rewarding. What we don't want to do is to read through all the pages and pages of terms

and conditions in order to obtain the reward."

In an op-ed in the New York Times on use of data, Google chief executive Sundar Pichai wrote: "First, data makes the products and services you use more helpful to you. It's what enables the Google Assistant to book a rental car for your trip … Second, products use anonymous data in aggregate to be more helpful to everyone."

Whistleblower Edward Snowden was horrified at the idea that people were happy to give away their most private of information. In his autobiography, Permanent Record, he recounts the first time he saw a smart fridge.

"I was convinced the only reason that thing was internet-equipped was so that it could report back to its manufacturer about its owner's usage and about any other household data that was obtainable. The manufacturer, in turn, would monetise that data by selling it. And we were supposed to pay for the privilege," he wrote.

It is not just in the USA that people are willing to share data. A 2018 survey by the Global Alliance of Data-Drive Marketing Associations of people in 10 countries showed that more than half of people decided whether to share their personal information on a case-by-case basis, dependent on the benefits.

Another problem is data creep. Many people sign up to use services with only a cursory glance at the lengthy terms and conditions, which often cover exactly what a company will do with your data.

This idea has become known as 'pay for privacy'

Microsoft's services agreement, for example, says, "…you grant Microsoft a worldwide and royalty-free intellectual property licence to use your content, for example, to make copies of, retain, transmit, reformat, distribute via communication tools and display your content on the services." That is pretty wide-ranging.

However, terms and conditions are not set in stone. Ashley Winton, a global data protection and privacy expert with law firm MWE, said in English contract law, normally you have to be aware of and agree to a change to the terms and conditions that apply to you. The laws in other countries are not so clear

Let's be clear: we can do more to make sure we are not giving away our private information, and companies can do more to make sure we know what we are giving away. Already the search engine Bing gives you a cut of the money it makes selling your data, offering Amazon vouchers for using it.

But Cyphers said: "The problem is that governments, and the US government in particular, have let the companies get enormously large without any serious regulation or even serious threats of consequences for bad behaviour. And that's a problem we can solve, both with strong privacy regulation and vigorous anti-trust enforcement to unwind some of the mergers that helped these firms grow so large."

Governments are keen to keep the flow of data coming. Oppressive governments who are addicted to the enormously intrusive insights that such data can bring on their opponents all the more so.

Something to think about next time you complacently click OK to sharing your information and location. ⊗

Mark Frary is a freelance journalist specialising in business and technology

Not my turf

Helen Lewis tells **Jemimah Steinfeld** how the vitriol aimed at people trying to discuss trans issues is feeding into the hands of the far right

49(01): 34/35 I DOI: 10.1177/0306422020917609

JOURNALIST **HELEN LEWIS** has joined an unenviable list of women who have been labelled Terfs (trans-exclusionary radical feminists) by people who disagree with them. But, as she tells Index, she's "neither a particularly radical feminist, nor am I trans-exclusionary". She was labelled with the term after arguing that gender self-identification was problematic in relation to rape shelters and women's changing rooms.

The term Terf, first coined in 2008, has taken on a life of its own in recent years. Like a heat-seeking missile, it races through the internet at breakneck speed, ready to smash into anyone who says the "wrong" thing in reference to trans people. Just ask JK Rowling and other women who have been labelled as Terfs. For Lewis, it's a term of sexist abuse; "a stain that's put on you".

"It's basically putting a label on somebody that says 'you don't have to listen to anything else this person has to say'."

The backlash has led to many people becoming wary of discussing anything related to trans issues.

"That has happened, I think, to trans people on both sides of the argument who – [and] obviously this is a very personal issue to them – have felt quite burned by it, but also to women and feminist campaigners and people who actually just want to find out more," she said.

Herein lies the problem. As many avoid the topic for fear of offending, the level of knowledge and understanding of trans lives, identity and experience is poor, says Lewis. And in this climate, where the middle ground is missing in action, anti-trans voices have more prominence than they should. "You see unsavoury people

[latching on to] the arguments and then you get exactly what happened in the immigration debate – a sense that there are big truths out that no one is allowed to say. Actually introducing some light onto that conversation would mean that those nasty bits wouldn't fester."

Lewis gives an example of the line that trans people are "innately predatory".

"[It] is pushed by unsavoury people on the far right and people get the sense that, because we are not allowed to talk about what happens in prisons (because that would get us in trouble), that maybe there is something in it, maybe there's something that we are not allowed to be told. Whereas having a sensible, grown-up conversation in the open would, I think and I hope, actually put those issues in perspective."

Lewis says that left-wing newspapers in particular are self-censoring. They have not been "harbouring any space for debate, acquiescing to the idea that any debate was in itself harmful and transphobic".

Lewis says she's aware of an internal debate at The Guardian among female staff members who feel that the issue hasn't been covered in a balanced way, although she says this is beginning to change (as evidenced by a recent article from Suzanne Moore). She also notes she has been lucky to have "bosses who always defended my right to write about difficult topics", but even then she says that in her past role as deputy editor at the New Statesman she was resented for publishing a range of views.

"People felt that only one view was acceptable," she said. She says many use the phrase "being on the right side of history"; and if

It's basically putting a label on somebody that says 'you don't have to listen to anything else this person has to say'

CREDIT: Patric Sandri/Ikon

people, particularly on social media, want to signal they are opposed to racism, sexism, homophobia or transphobia, they find an opinion which makes their case and then parrot it without necessarily engaging with the details.

So where does all this leave the average person?

"If you're a random schoolteacher or cleaner or civil servant, why have an opinion on a subject that could lead to complaints against you to your professional body, could lead you getting censored by your employer, could lead to you ending up on a site on the internet with a label against you?" she said.

And people are also reluctant to engage if it could threaten their jobs, as was seen in the case of Maya Forstater, a tax expert whose contract was not renewed at a charity last year following comments she made on Twitter about transgender identity.

"If it's not a life or death issue to you immediately, [you] think, 'why stick my neck out?'. I know academics who have had complaints to their professional unions, people try to 'no platform' them," she said.

She adds that event hosts might also try to programme an event on the condition that there is a balance of views – someone in favour of self-identification and someone against – but they can't find anyone to speak in favour "because they say they won't appear on a platform with 'transphobes', so the whole event gets cancelled".

Of course, name-calling and women turning on women isn't unique to those discussing trans issues. Lewis, whose book Difficult Women: A History of Feminism in 11 Fights was published this February, is all too familiar with how women can be their own worst enemies.

Of the feminist movement specifically, she says: "Any movement ends up with hierarchies

and interpersonal rivalries… I don't know why we would ever think that feminism, because it's mostly women, would be immune to forces that are pretty much constant across all of human life and hierarchical organisations."

Rather than condemning those who choose to remain silent, Lewis is sympathetic. "It's a difficult thing to put yourself at odds with the prevailing culture."

Jemimah Steinfeld is deputy editor of Index on Censorship

49(01): 36/37 I DOI: 10.1177/03064220209217610

MARTIN ROWSON
is a cartoonist for
The Guardian and
the author of various
books, including
The Communist
Manifesto (2018), a
graphic novel adap-
tion of the famous
19th century book

Driven towards the exit

Government influence within Bulgaria's media has seen a number of high-profile journalists pushed out of their jobs, says **Victoria Pavlova**

49(01): 38/40 I DOI: 10.1177/0306422020917611

HAIL A TAXI on the streets of Sofia and you might get the surprise of finding that your driver is Miroluba Benatova, who until recently was one of the most famous investigative reporters on Bulgarian television.

Benatova was regularly seen on screen and is best known for her eponymous investigative programmes looking into organ harvesting, trafficking of children and political corruption, among other issues.

The journalist, who in 2011 was voted one of Bulgaria's most influential women by Capital magazine, says cab driving affords her a different perspective on life in the country.

"Driving lets me speak to tens of people a day and lets me see how they interpret the media narrative," Benatova said.

Since June, she has been using her social media platform to retell the personal stories of everyday people, impacted by the rampant corruption in the country.

"I can't predict how the media environment will develop over the next few years," she said.

"But at the moment, media content is completely synchronised with the government's narrative. There are no dissenting voices. And,

yes, this worries me. This warped media environment influences all of society."

Benatova believes her rapid fall out of the limelight was spurred by a change in ownership at her employer Nova Broadcasting Group, the country's second largest national media network, in March last year. The group was acquired by brothers Kiril and Georgi Domuschiev – wealthy industrialists with documented ties to Prime Minister Boyko Borisov and members of his administration – through their Advance Media Group. In June, Benatova was told she would have to accept new terms of employment, known in the business as a "rejection offer", effectively making her freelance.

"I was offered a switch to a civil contract – essentially a freelance arrangement – where I was to pitch pieces and the network has the freedom to accept or reject them," she said.

She believes the proposed contract change was linked to the content of some of her reports making uncomfortable viewing for the new owners.

"I received pushback from the network for a brief interview with [then Bulgarian MP] Tsvetan Tsvetanov," recalled Benatova. "The original investigation wasn't mine, but the network didn't approve of certain questions I asked."

The investigation in question implicated Tsvetanov in a corruption scandal, which saw him, alongside family members, acquire six properties in Sofia between 2004 and 2009. Benatova was not investigating anything particularly controversial when she was asked to switch contracts. "But overall, my journalistic profile did not correspond to the new editorial direction."

The personnel changes have continued into 2020. On 30 January, Nova confirmed the departure of caricaturist Valdes Radev, known for his sharp critiques of the government.

At the moment, media content is completely synchronised with the government's narrative. There are no dissenting voices

Radev's contract was cancelled by Nova. A day later, journalist and anchor Lora Krumova announced her resignation, motivated by "processes at the network".

The year-long reshuffle began with the hiring of Milyana Veleva in May 2019 from Kanal 3, a news network controlled by MP Delyan Peevski.

"The current leadership of Nova is completely insensitive to the standards of independent journalism and shows all signs of a plant, rather than an actual owner," states a prominent Bulgarian journalist who has been covering the personnel changes since they began. The journalist requested not to be named.

"It is very clear to see that the news and reporting division is controlled by associates of Delyan Peevski."

Benatova was not alone in being handed a rejection offer by Nova. At the same time, Genka Shikerova and Marin Nikolov. veteran investigative reporters with the group, were told they were being made freelance.

Faced with this demotion, the two journalists resigned, preferring to look for work elsewhere. Shikerova left the network that month while Nikolov left in September.

"The conditions of my new contract were intended to make me resign – they were designed to make it impossible for me to continue working for Nova," said Shikerova.

Nikolov stated that, in the conversation between him, Shikerova and Veleva, the network executive cited diminished productivity – fewer segments produced by Nova's investigative team between 2018 and early 2019.

"I can't comment on the motivations of the network, but after 15 years with the network, the sudden offer of a change in contract felt like

a lack of recognition for my work at the very least," Nikolov said.

When asked about the reasons behind the 2019 and 2020 reshuffles, a Nova representative stated that "there were no firings in 2019". The network did not respond to further questions.

This move is part of a pattern of what anti-censorship body Reporters Without Borders (RSF) describes as rampant "corruption and collusion between media, politicians and oligarchs" in Bulgaria. RSF annually publishes a World Press Freedom Index. In 2006, Bulgaria ranked 36 out of 180 countries in the index. By 2019, it had dropped to 111, the lowest position of any EU country.

This happened amid a series of assassinations and attempted assassinations of journalists and a wave of cost-cuts that left a number of veteran journalists unemployed, as well as the distinct lack of media pluralism.

This happened amid a series of assassinations and attempted assassinations of journalists

→ It also happened in an environment where politicians think it is fair game to mock and threaten journalists. This February, for example, RSF called on the authorities to stop trying to intimidate journalists after Borisov likened them – especially women journalists – to turkeys during a press conference. "And then, in a surreal attempt to mock them, tried to imitate the gobbling of a turkey for several seconds, ignoring the protests of the journalists present," RSF said in a statement.

While some journalists welcome a change to freelance status, for many it can mean they lose valuable protections enjoyed by employed staff, and it can lead to financial insecurity. As well as driving a cab, Benatova also writes online features for several outlets in order to scrape by. Meanwhile, Shikerova continues her reporting work, producing investigative pieces, but she is frequently out of pocket.

"[During an investigative project] we calculated how much tickets, hotels and travel would cost, and the media group covered these post-factum," Shikerova explained.

"Broadcast reporting on a freelance basis is impossible. These are boutique productions, because the production of video content is expensive. This is not a functional business model – it isn't sustainable."

The Union of Bulgarian Journalists – an affiliate of the European Federation of Journalists – has expressed concern over the changes at Nova.

"We are worried about the proposition to change the working status of the aforementioned investigative journalists and their effective transition to freelancing arrangements, offering their productions to the network," the organisation said.

"This gives the network the power to accept or reject proposed investigations, and implies that during the course of their work, the journalists represent only themselves and do not have the defence of an authoritative media."

Lada Price, a lecturer in journalism at Sheffield Hallam University in the UK, said: "The traditional business model for mainstream media, not just in Bulgaria but in many other countries, is under threat and most are finding it hard to survive from sales and advertising.

"The global financial crisis in 2008-09 made the situation worse. The crisis allowed the oligarchs to gain more influence. The German publisher WAZ left Bulgaria in 2010 mostly because of the intertwining of politics and economics, according to its owners. Bulgaria is the most corrupt country in the European Union and that has a negative impact on media and journalism. One of the main problems is that nobody knows who's behind the media, who finances them. It is no surprise that trust in the media is so low." ⊗

Victoria Pavlova is a freelance journalist from Varna, Bulgaria

ABOVE: Miroluba Benatova next to the taxi she drives after losing her contract as a full time investigative journalist

Shadowing the golden age of Soviet censorship

Turkmen writer-in-exile **Ak Welsapar** says that while Soviet-era censorship was strict it is nothing compared to what is happening in Turkmenistan today. Back then, at least, censorship had a human face

49(01): 41/43 I DOI: 10.1177/0306422020917612

SINCE INDEPENDENCE, TURKMENISTAN has become a second North Korea and censorship has painted national literature and art as both harmful and hostile.

Today, Turkmenistan is ruled by Gurbanguly Berdimuhamedov, a former dentist who rose to the lofty position of health minister under his predecessor, the dictator Saparmurat Niyazov, who took to styling himself as Turkmenbashi, or head of the Turkmen.

Under Berdimuhamedov, Turkmen's censors have been given carte blanche. Internet access is only available through the state provider Turkmentelecom and is one of the most expensive and slowest in the world. Today only one fifth of the population of Turkmenistan can access the internet.

All popular social media platforms, including YouTube, Facebook, Telegram and WhatsApp, are completely blocked. Those who try to evade the ban can expect three to five years in prison. Even when abroad, Turkmen citizens are afraid to visit opposition websites, as any disobedience leads to the immediate detention of their relatives in the country.

Yet one writer has been incredibly profilic in the Berdimuhamedov era and that is the Turkmen president himself. He has managed to "create" more than 60 books over the past 10 years.

In this he follows in the literary footsteps of his predecessor Niyazov who was also the only permitted writer. Nizayov's most infamous work is his book of preachings, Ruhnama.

Censorship in Turkmenistan today is even stricter than in the bad old days of the Soviet Union.

Just like sex, there was never censorship in the USSR – no one talked about either. And yet there was Glavlit, the general directorate for literature and publishing. Established in 1922 by decree of the Council of People's Commissars, Glavlit was entrusted with "the preliminary review of all works and other printed materials intended for publication" and made official gatekeeper of the "list of information prohibited for publication in open press,

RIGHT: A statue in Ashgabat, capital of Turkmenistan, celebrates former dictator Niyazov's infamous book Ruhnama

Just like sex, there was never censorship in the USSR – no one talked about either

→ radio and television programmes".

Glavlit was intended to protect communist ideals from criticism and sheltered millions of Soviet people from free thinking, tantamount to thoughtcrime. The very name Glavlit echoes Massolit, from the satirical novel by the great Mikhail Bulgakov, The Master and Margarita. In the book, Massolit – a corrupt trade union for writers whose name stands for "literature for the masses" – is satirised for its excesses.

Perhaps ironically, Bulgakov himself, along with such writers as Babel, Pilnyak, Zamyatin, Fedin, Zoshchenko, Leskov and Merezhkovsky, drew the special attention of Glavlit.

Soviet writers achieved breathtaking heights in world literature despite the best efforts of Glavlit, although what was published was largely adapted from the original.

Censorship, a KGB responsibility, could permanently cure the itch of disobedience from most writers. A few stubborn truth-lovers either ended up in correctional camps, like Osip Mandelstam, or were incarcerated for life in mental hospitals, like the Turkmen poetess Annasoltan Kekilova, or were forced into exile, such as Aleksandr Solzhenitsyn, Iosif Brodsky and Vladimir Voynovich.

In Soviet-era Turkmenistan, for instance, one could not say that the Turkmens had written before the Bolshevik revolution, even though they had a rich tradition of literature. It was also impossible to write the truth about the bloody conquest of the Turkmen land by the tsars. Instead, it was recommended to speak only of how the country had voluntarily joined the USSR.

I described these obvious discrepancies in my novel The Melon Head. It won a prestigious prize in 1984 in the Closed Literary Contest but had to wait until 1988 to be published – and even then only thanks to the policy of perestroika. Glavlit did not want the novel's themes of undermining the foundations of Soviet society to shake the trust of ordinary people in Soviet power.

Not all writers had the courage to defend their work. Plenty got on well with the communist regime, choosing a quiet life instead of fighting for justice. For example, the leadership of the Writers' Union in Moscow consisted entirely of writers who made a voluntary deal with the communist authorities – a Faustian pact subordinating their talents to the strict ideological requirements of the regime. These writers served the Soviet regime in exchange for profitable positions, awards and material goods.

Censors did sometimes favour the authors in places where the harm of their words was not proven. This, together with the occasional good-natured censor, sometimes caused unprecedented upsurges in Soviet literature.

I remember the effect of the novel The Day Lasts More Than a Hundred Years by the great Kyrgyz-Russian writer Chinghiz Aitmatov. It talked about the time of Joseph Stalin's repressions, but the reader could easily extrapolate this into the 1970s and the first half of the 1980s when totalitarianism prevailed.

It is not surprising, therefore, that my preferred literary style – magical realism – was formed as protection against censorship. When perestroika started and the USSR dissolved, my books started to be published.

Censorship – which did not exist – was finally abolished by the Supreme Soviet of the USSR's Law On Press and Other Mass Media; it decreed that "censorship of mass media is not allowed".

Yet this openness was shortlived and worse was to come – the national Turkmen censor was established in the same year as the dissolution of the USSR and, mirroring the old Soviet tradition,

It was at that moment that I realised that literature and art in Turkmenistan were over for the foreseeable future

a donkey." The healer asks what sort of donkey it was. "Why, a Turkmen-Soviet donkey!" The censor banned this and other funny episodes, leaving almost no life in the text.

In an attempt to save the mangled text, I asked to see the head of Turkmenistan's offical censorship body, who had been a communist functionary throughout his career. He explained Turkmen-Soviet donkeys did not exist in nature. The censor did not understand – or did not want to understand – any of my arguments on metaphors and allegories in literature.

I asked for a list of forbidden topics to help me write within the rules. The answer upset me: "We do not have any list. President Niyazov fully trusts us. We decide for ourselves what to allow and what not to allow."

It was at that moment that I realised that literature and art in Turkmenistan were over for the foreseeable future. No one can ever get around censorship without rules.

Soon my fears were confirmed: the Writers' Union and the Academy of Sciences of Turkmenistan were disbanded, libraries in villages and district centres were closed, books were scrapped.

Only those Turkmen writers who left the country for political reasons, as I did, have not given up hope for a bright future for Turkmen literature. ⊗

LEFT: Turkmenistan's former dictator Saparmurat Niyazov Turkmenbashi

Turkmen censorship was not acknowledged.

Eventually the censor took offence to my articles on infant and maternal mortality in Turkmenistan caused by the super-chemicalisation of agriculture and the drying-up of the Aral Sea and the publication of my books stopped.

I must admit I preferred the "human face" of the late Soviet censorship.

In late 1991, my satirical novel A Curve of a Sabre Hanging on an Old Carpet was printed in the bilingual magazine Yashlyk-Yunost, subject to censorship by the national authorities. The censor especially disliked that its characters kept dislocating their arms and sought help not from a doctor but from the village bone healer. In one episode, a man is asked how he managed to dislocate it. He answers: "I fell off

Ak Welsapar is an award-winning Swedish-Turkmen writer with a PhD in philosophy

Silent majority

Stefano Pozzebon talks to frightened and
tired Venezuelans, who wonder if
anything will ever change

49(01): 44/46 I DOI: 10.1177/0306422020917613

APRIL IS A month of reflection for the
Venezuelan opposition movement. In April
2002, a coup briefly toppled the late President
Hugo Chavez, only to end in failure and leave
the populist leader stronger than ever. Last
year, opposition leader Juan Guaido declared a
military insurrection against President Nicolas
Maduro, but the revolt was stopped in its
tracks. This year, any rebellious spirit seems to
have been simply sucked away.

Like many other authoritarian leaders across
the world, Maduro rules thanks to a mix of
brutal repression, political shrewdness and
control of information. Many Venezuelans
have long stopped believing that Maduro's days
could end soon, and are adjusting to the new
reality of living in a totalitarian society: keep
your mouth shut or go somewhere else. For
those who don't want to join the almost five
million Venezuelans who have already left, not
saying anything about anything becomes the
only way to cope.

"There are at least three types of self-censorship in Venezuela," said Luis Carlos Diaz,
a Spanish-Venezuelan journalist, human rights
activist and online media expert.

There are the journalists who cannot cover
a story because of a lack of information, the
shutdown of access to government institutions, or physical impossibility to do their job.
(Blackouts and roadblocks have become the
norm in most of Venezuela outside the largest
urban areas.)

Another type, according to Diaz, is self-
censorship due to polarisation: an activist or a
journalist may not want to denounce something
that may damage the political side they feel

aligned with. That is why you don't see
pro-government media covering opposition
marches, and vice-versa.

This type of self-censorship is common
not only in Venezuela but also in many
other deeply polarised countries, and increasingly so. One of the battle cries of the
wave of protests that rocked Latin America
last year, from Chile to Bolivia to Colombia,
was that the government media would not
attend the protests for political reasons.

But the third, and most common, type
of self-censorship is the one motivated by
preservation and triggered by fear.

It is the most common because it touches not
only reporters and pro-
fessionals but also wider
society, which tacitly
understands that the
consequences for speak-
ing up, or not following
the rules, are dire.

One case is par-
ticularly telling. Jesus
Medina, a photo-
journalist, served 16
months in a military
jail after posting a
video directed at Chav-
ismo radical leader
Diosdado Cabello.

Medina is explicitly
anti-Maduro. On 28
August 2018, he argued
that the people who
lived in Caracas's
largest slum, Petare,
should protest against
the government. The
following day, he was
detained by agents of
Maduro's secret police,
the Bolivarian Service
of National Intelligence
(SEBIN).

His lawyer, Stefania
Migliorini, says the
agents did not have an
arrest order to detain

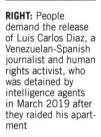

RIGHT: People
demand the release
of Luis Carlos Diaz, a
Venezuelan-Spanish
journalist and human
rights activist, who
was detained by
intelligence agents
in March 2019 after
they raided his apart-
ment

Medina, that he was psychologically tortured while under custody, and that the agents took him to a military jail outside Caracas, Ramo Verde.

Medina was charged with five counts, ranging from money laundering to incitement. Two of the charges were dropped before the trial even began. As Medina was kept in jail under precautionary arrest, the hearings were repeatedly postponed. After spending more than 16 months in prison, Medina was granted house arrest on 6 January this year. His trial finally began on 30 January, 488 days after his initial detention.

Medina has no doubt about why he was detained: "The Venezuelan state was looking

They have cameras and hidden microphones all over the place

for an example to scare the others and, among other journalists, I have always been a symbol against censorship."

Data from human rights organisations show that brutality is growing, especially during the intense street clashes that took over Venezuela in 2017 and 2019.

The companies they work for could be wiped away if they publish information beyond what is expected

→ In 2018, Espacio Publico, a human rights watchdog, registered 608 violations of freedom of expression. In the first eight months alone of 2019, there were 845 violations, the vast majority in the first four months of protests, culminating with Guaido's uprising.

Professional journalists know that the companies they work for could be wiped away if they publish information beyond what is expected.

"In a way, the channel has to look after itself," said a national TV channel correspondent, who asked to speak to Index anonymously for fear of retaliation.

"Of course, it's not ideal, I know that. It's not ideal, and it's not what we learnt at school, but this is the reality."

Public employees often feel they are directly in the line of fire: around 30 were victims of retaliation, threats and persecution for taking part in opposition protests and denouncing corruption, according to Espacio Publico.

Marisol Chirinos, a worker at public oil company PDVSA, doesn't use social media because she fears her accounts would be monitored by PDVSA internal security which, she says, employs former SEBIN officers. Many of her colleagues use pseudonyms on Twitter or Instagram.

"We stay away from expressing our views at work," she said, "but they have cameras and hidden microphones all over the place. We are pawns in the hands of the state as long as we work there."

The PDVSA press team did not reply to a request to respond to the allegations that the company's employees were spied upon.

Given that Chirinos's salary is less than £10 ($12) a month, one would ask if it is really worth keeping her mouth shut, but she said: "It's our stability at stake. I don't want to get into trouble."

Terror and people's desire for a quiet life are being used to blunt free speech. "People self-censor really a lot here," said Luz Mely Reyes, founder of the online portal Efecto Cocuyo and one of the most famous journalists in Venezuela.

"The classic thing," she explained, "is that they say: 'I can tell you, but don't put my name'. And you can see why: by our reckoning, there have been 17 people arrested here for a tweet."

Diaz, the human rights activist, agrees: "This is a sadistic state. There is no symmetry, rather a completely disproportionate use of force. Officers in balaclavas use weapons against private citizens."

Diaz has also faced the weight of the government repression. On 11 March 2019, he was detained by SEBIN and taken to a clandestine prison before being released the following day after intense diplomatic pressure from Spain.

On top of the repressive apparatus stands Maduro himself, who is the first to benefit from the lack of expressed dissent.

People are not proud to be swallowing their emotions but sadly, as fewer people open their mouths, the wall of silence grows stronger.

"Many people say that as long as we, the public employees, don't speak out, nothing will change," said Chirinos. "Deep down, I keep hoping that one day I will be able to see my boss face to face and tell him what is wrong at the company, I do. But right now, my level of hope is close to zero."

Reyes, who remembers working as a journalist in the pre-Chavez days, is quick to highlight a more sinister risk of the silencing culture: "The ultimate risk is that now the opposition leaders demand the same… After seeing that the Chavistas have got away with it for 20 years, I fear that once Maduro finally falls, the next round of politicians ruling the country will be just as intolerant against those who think differently." ⊗

Stefano Pozzebon is a journalist and regular contributor to Index, based in Caracas, Venezuela

Academically challenged

Kaya Genç talks to Turkish academics on why they said nothing while their colleagues were sacked and imprisoned

49(01): 47/49 I DOI: 10.1177/0306422020917614

TURKISH SCHOLARS HAVE been forced into a form of ideological complicity in order to survive in academia. Since the clampdown on civil liberties began in 2017 after the coup, scholars feel they have to parrot the government line and inform on their colleagues, and even campaign for their imprisonment, just to keep their own jobs. But there are lines that even the most conflict-averse will not cross.

Anıl Özgüç, a professor of medicine at Istanbul's Aydın University, and a contributor to progressive website T24, found herself in the eye of a Mephistophelian storm recently. As a medical scholar, she had long stayed silent about politics in the workplace.

"Then one morning I woke up to find my name printed in all the national newspapers as a signatory of a petition I'd not signed," Özgüç told Index.

"The petition demanded the imprisonment of scholars who had signed a 'Peace Petition'. I was traumatised to see my name attached to it. I can't describe the sadness I felt that morning: first there was shame, and then anger."

Özgüç's silence had begun in January 2016 when 1,128 scholars issued the Peace Petition, asking for a ceasefire in the war between Turkish security forces and armed militant group the PKK. Noam Chomsky, David Harvey and Judith Butler, as well as leading Turkish scholars, were among the signatories. Soon after the Turkish government accused signatories of defending terrorism and opened a court case, the number of signatories snowballed to 2,212.

The petition was forwarded to Özgüç as well. But she didn't sign it. "I didn't feel safe with all its content," she recalled. "I had lots of friends who signed it. They lost their jobs, their health and their future. I still feel like crying when I think of what they've been through."

Thousands of scholars continued working and kept their mouths shut. They refrained from talking about taboo subjects, such as the Kurdish question, because of social pressure, persuaded that this would result in more security. Meanwhile, their colleagues were detained after dawn raids on their homes, or were forced to flee for their safety.

But in 2019, Turkey's Constitutional Court annulled the convictions and the courts began releasing those who had been imprisoned. For scholars such as Özgüç, who sympathised with their cause, this was happy news. Department heads hoped colleagues would return from exile to their teaching posts. Nobody quite expected what happened next.

On 20 July 2019, pro-government scholars published their own petition, The Constitutional Court Can't Legitimise Terror. Signed by 1,071 scholars, it described the court's decision "concerning the rights abuses of some scholars who have propagated terror in their so-called Peace Petition" as "scandalous".

The decision "has hurt the memory of our martyrs and wounded the public conscience", the petitioners said. "Finding fault with the state for its struggle against terrorism can't be categorised as freedom of expression, anywhere in the world."

Özgüç's name was among the signatories despite her not having seen the petition, let

---

I've built little pockets of freedom at school where I can remain optimistic and embrace my students

→ alone signing it. The campaign seemed like a test of their willingness to remain silent.

But this attempt at continued coercion has had the opposite effect, and scholars have begun to raise their voices. Mehmet Şerif Eskin, a literature professor from Istanbul University who wasn't outspoken about politics in the past, started a campaign to clear his name. He said he didn't hear about the petition before seeing his name on its signatory list.

"This is a shameful thing," he said. "How could they use my signature without asking me?"

Another professor, Ercan Eyüboğlu, from Aydın University, tweeted: "I deplore those friends who believe that I could've signed such a petition!" He summarised his feelings in three words: "rebellion, indignation, fury". Soon the number of names on the petition dropped to 1,068.

Like other silenced scholars, the petition was the last straw for Özgüç. She resigned from her post the following morning. She says she realised how freedom and security were indistinguishable for her: "Being forced to pick one destroys our souls." She regrets her past inaction and silent agreement with scholars who, "in order to feel safe, told themselves: 'I'd better stay silent. If I can manage not to see upsetting things around me, then I won't be upset by them'." She says such magical thinking isn't part of only academic life. "What we experienced mirrors the whole society."

Her regret was a common utterance. Many also felt anger, guilt and resentment that they had chosen to stay silent but had still, ultimately, fallen foul of the system.

Paradoxically, while Özgüç – who did not sign the original Peace Petition – wants scholars to be more outspoken, Sarphan Uzunoğlu, who

did sign it, asks for caution.

"Self-censorship for my betterment is part of my daily routine," he confessed in an interview with Index, questioning whether the petition which led to his prosecution was useful at all, considering its outcome.

"Many students were deprived of the good influence those scholars might have had on them had they not lost their jobs after signing the petition," he said.

A lecturer at Kadir Has University and the editor of website NewsLabTurkey, he believes "unthinking deals of silence" are part of the social contract the "post-truth political order" imposes on us. It is "almost impossible" to have a balance between the struggle for freedom and the comfort of security, he argues. "What defines Turkish academia is self-censorship, rather than censorship."

Uzunoğlu describes a chilling atmosphere of coercion in Turkish colleges where students record their teachers in lessons and during visits to their office, and scholars inform on their colleagues. But he says this atmosphere should make us more, rather than less, tolerant of scholars who have little choice other than submission: "Under these circumstances, nobody should accuse those who prioritise security and safety."

Fighting coercion, Özgüç says, may increasingly become a privilege available only to those who wield power in academia. When she faced hostility from the pro-government press after speaking out about removing her signature, colleagues assured Özgüç she would be safe once she became an assistant professor. "This sounds childish but is a reality nevertheless," she said. "There is a pattern of seeking protection for free expression through academic titles."

> *Uzunoğlu describes a chilling atmosphere of coercion in Turkish colleges where students record their teachers in lessons*

Such stories resemble what Turkish media experienced half a decade ago, when many newspaper editors and television presenters sustained a strategic silence in order to keep their jobs. During 2013's popular protests at Istanbul's Gezi Park, CNN Turk showed a documentary on penguins; the editor of the news division who made that call, a committed Marxist, has since apologised. Like many of his colleagues, he no longer works in the mainstream media.

"I've built little pockets of freedom at school where I can remain optimistic and embrace my students," Özgüç said. "But I'm not sure if that amounts to real academic freedom."

Uzunoğlu agrees. Individual responses are insufficient in fighting the overriding coercive atmosphere. "Universities are un-unionised, so scholars lack protection. Even if we have a new government, these problems would remain,

since they're integral to the way our universities work." (Unions do exist but their power is limited. In fact, some have been attacked, such as the Eğitim-Sen union. While Eğitim-Sen has thousands of members it has had to fight court cases for, respectively, defending the Kurdish language and secularism. Membership to Eğitim-Sen and other unions may therefore actually add to the precarious sitations of Turkish scholars.)

And yet, he argues, Turkish scholars wouldn't be persuaded so easily to give up part of their freedom in exchange for their security if they had the backing of institutional protections. That's something they should fight for. ⊗

Kaya Genç is a contributing editor to Index on Censorship. He lives in Istanbul

Unhealthy market

As China struggles to recover its economy after the coronavirus, **Charlotte Middlehurst** asks will this alter pressure on foreign companies to censor content before operating within its borders

49(01): 50/52 | DOI: 10.1177/0306422020917615

THE LEGACY OF the coronavirus in the country where it all began is likely to continue long after the virus itself subsides. The Chinese government may have seen some push-back from its citizens on how it initially managed information surrounding the outbreak, but at the end of the crisis it might find itself with even more control over how information is disseminated within its borders.

"Beijing is trying to balance a tightening of social control in the interest of public health, and a loosening of social control to promote economic growth. Loosening social control means encouraging companies and people to go back to work," said William Callahan, a professor of international relations at LSE.

"However, China is unlikely to loosen its control over censorship – even for international companies like Apple – to promote economic activity.

"From what we've seen, Beijing is using the coronavirus crisis to build and enforce a more intense surveillance and control regime. This goes beyond censorship to produce and promote 'positive news' about China's efforts to fight the pandemic, alongside 'negative news' that criticises how Italy, the USA and other countries deal with it."

Aynne Kokos, assistant professor at the department of media studies, University of Virginia, said: "I think there will be a slight loosening of inbound investment restrictions to support economic recovery. However, all indications suggest that the information environment will actually be more tightly controlled."

"Whether or not the coronavirus dents China's image depends on how successfully other countries respond as well as what happens when people in China return to work," she said

Christina Maags, lecturer in Chinese politics at SOAS, University of London, said: "While the Chinese economy is suffering losses, it is also multi-national companies like Apple who are eager to find a quick solution so as to stop the delay in production and resulting negative impact on supply chains worldwide. Therefore, I think Xi and multinational companies both have interests in "reviving" the Chinese economy."

The world can only wait to see whether China will be more inclined to encourage economic activity after the coronavirus outbreak, or things stay the same. Previously the importance that the authorities have placed on managing information has led to dozens of prominent brands issuing public apologies in China over recent years, a sign of how powerful the Chinese government has become. Household names accused of bending to Chinese pressure range from Marvel Studios, for featuring a Tibetan monk in an animation (the screenwriter later changed the character after acknowledging the company "risked alienating a billion people" who did not recognise Tibet as a place), to gaming group Red Candle,

The world can only wait to see whether China will be more desperate to encourage economic activity after the coronavirus outbreak, or things stay the same

which included artwork comparing President Xi Jinping with Winnie the Pooh in one of its games (Xi is known to take offence to such comparisons). Meanwhile, catwalk brands Versace and Givenchy felt the need to say sorry for recognising Taiwan as a country.

China's influence over foreign companies seeking access to its consumer market has been growing over the past few years. But those who trade freedom for profit run the risk of reputational damage among consumers who care about the consequences of reneging on free speech.

"The Chinese government has become more aggressive in getting foreign companies to comply with whatever foreign demands they have and silencing people," said Yaqiu Wang, a senior researcher at Human Rights Watch. "By caving into the Chinese demands you are putting your values [aside] – social responsibility, freedom. It is really corrosive. You are affecting global freedom of speech."

Companies that comply with Chinese demands risk setting dangerous precedents and make it easier for other national leaders to exact similar demands. Apple, which has come under fire for supporting the Chinese government during the Hong Kong protests, has recently been criticised in India after censoring its local Apple TV programmes, just as freedom

of speech and assembly is being threatened under Prime Minister Narendra Modi.

During the coronavirus outbreak China has been doubling down on its censorship of online forums as it seeks to control narratives around the disease. On 31 December, a day after doctors tried to warn the public about the then unknown virus, YY, a live-streaming platform, added 45 words to its blacklist, according to Citizen Lab. WeChat, a messaging app with a billion users, also censored coronavirus-related content.

They say they are simply complying with local laws when we all know what they really care about is market access

→ Censored material included references to Li Wenliang, a doctor who had been silenced by police for trying to warn about the virus, and neutral references to efforts on handling the outbreak.

The death of Li started a digital uprising (#WeWantFreedomOfSpeech), with people calling for online censorship to be lifted.

Kevin Latham, senior lecturer in social anthropology at the SOAS, University of London, China Institute, said: "The narrative on censorship has shifted over the weeks a bit. At the beginning it was clear they were much more open and quicker to act publicly than with Sars in the past – they appeared to have learned that lesson.

"However, once the story about the death of Li Wenliang came out, that narrative was undermined to some degree."

What's the story so far? Apple blocks more than 370 apps in China, according to Chinese security experts Great Fire, including the virtual proxy networks that allow people to vault over firewalls. The company has failed to lift restrictions despite renewed pressure arising during the pandemic. Its decision to block a map app used by protesters in Hong Kong, taken a few months before, was also called out by critics.

Apple chief executive Tim Cook has defended the decision as borne of legal necessity.

"We would obviously rather not remove the apps but, like we do in other countries, we follow the law wherever we do business," he said in 2017. "We strongly believe participating in markets and bringing benefits to customers is in the best interest of the folks there and in other countries as well."

Wang said: "They say they are simply complying with local laws when we all know what they really care about is market access."

Apple is not the only tech company criticised for capitulation. In 2018 Google tried to build its own filtered search engine for China but the idea was scrapped following an outcry from its employees.

Jeremy Daum, a senior research scholar at Yale Law School, says that while strict laws do exist, many statutes are written in a vague and sweeping manner, so it can be hard to know what the legal obligations really are. "In some cases it can be as vague as not publishing content that harms the nation's interests," he said.

Daum highlights the importance of distinguishing between enforced censorship and corporate acquiescence. "Complicity sounds like they share a common goal of censorship, [but] the companies' goals are profit, so they are not complicit in motive – it's acquiescence," he said.

The challenges to the power dynamic will centre on China's influence to change content coming from beyond its borders. Apple TV+ has already issued guidelines to its programme makers to avoid portraying China in a bad light.

Ultimately, harming freedom of expression hits society's most vulnerable, and those with the weakest voices, the most. "Censorship isn't just about politics," said Karen Reilly, a community director at GreatFire.org, which tracks censorship in China.

"Censorship blocks people from reaching their communities and this is especially harmful to marginalised and young people. Online spaces are sources of support. If you grow up with censorship, your connection to your own culture may be cut off." ⊗

*Additional research by **Orna Herr** and **Adam Aiken***

*****Charlotte Middlehurst** is a London-based journalist specialising in China. She tweets at @charmiddle*

When silence is not enough

If you fail to speak out, are you complicit in accepting what is going on? **Julian Baggini** thinks out loud

49(01): 53/55 I DOI: 10.1177/0306422020917616

"**W**HAT'S HAPPENING?" ASKS Twitter, inviting me to tweet. I carefully craft my 245 characters. Then I hesitate. Select all. Cut. I paste the tweet into a note, unsent.

It's not that I doubt the truth and importance of those few words. It's simply that if I post them I might become a target for trolls, and an organisation I work for could also come under fire. It's not worth the hassle. Or at least that's how it seems. But I worry. Has my self-censorship made me complicit in a suppression of free speech and the promotion of a viewpoint I believe needs challenging?

The idea that silence equals complicity has become popular wisdom, with Einstein and Martin Luther King among those quoted endorsing it. At an exhibition by a pro-Palestinian group, one of the volunteers told me: "If we don't do anything about this injustice, we're complicit in it."

It's powerful rhetoric, but it cannot be right. There are innumerable injustices around the world. Save for a handful of full-time activists and professionals in organisations such as Index, the finite supply of time ensures that most of us are silent about the vast majority of them.

Still, there are sins of omission. Not speaking up about one of thousands of injustices unconnected to you is not the same as keeping quiet about one happening under your very nose. I remember such a situation when I was a student working over the Christmas holidays at a Children's World store. In a break, one of the staff told a young female British Asian employee that he was racist. It was an odd exchange, without menace or overt hostility, but still completely unacceptable.

A few of us were there. None of us said anything, no doubt telling ourselves that he was a crank, very possibly drunk, and wasn't actually causing anyone harm. But I look back with shame at my silence. By keeping quiet we all implicitly endorsed the idea that what he said was within the realm of acceptable speech. We also failed to reassure a fellow employee from a group which commonly faced discrimination that we were fully on her side, no doubt adding to her discomfort.

A powerful tool to help understand this is the philosopher J.L. Austin's concept of a "speech act". The key idea is very simple: words do not only convey information, they can actually do things. When a boss says "You're fired", a person loses their job. When a male manager says something misogynistic, he diminishes the status of female colleagues and makes their opinions count for less.

I'm not sure if Austin ever talked about the corollary of speech acts: acts of silence. When people do things with words, the way others react can either counter or reinforce this. In both my examples, imagine that a more senior (male) manager is there. By speaking he can cancel the dismissal or pull up the colleague on his misogyny. Both speech acts change the effects of the first.

If, however, he is silent, he endorses the primary speech acts and allows to happen things that he could easily stop. Remaining silent can be an act one chooses to do, with consequences.

With distant injustices, things are different. When a lone citizen says nothing about, →

Not speaking up about one of thousands of injustices unconnected to you is not the same as keeping quiet

CREDIT: Lee Woodgate/Ikon

say, the plight if the Uyghurs in China, this has negligible endorsing or tolerating effect. When we are face to face with an injustice, however, silence can not only be a form of complicity, it can also serve to bolster wrongdoing.

This is what I fear I did when I deleted my tweet. It was triggered by responses to a tweet by JK Rowling in December 2019:

"Dress however you please.

Call yourself whatever you like.

Sleep with any consenting adult who'll have you.

Live your best life in peace and security.

But force women out of their jobs for stating that sex is real?

#IStandWithMaya #ThisIsNotADrill"

The hashtag "IStandWithMaya" referred to the case of Maya Forstater, whose contract with a think-tank was not renewed after she made a series of tweets opposing government plans to reform the Gender Recognition Act. This would allow people to self-identify as the opposite sex. The most notorious of these tweets stated "Men cannot change into women".

Transgender rights have become some of the most bitterly contested issues of our time. Yet the nub of the disagreement is not about the rights of trans people to live their lives free from prejudice and discrimination. It is between those who insist that it is entirely the individual's choice which sex they are and those who insist that there are also objective, biological considerations.

Those who maintain that biology has a role call themselves "gender critical" feminists while their opponents dismiss them as "Terfs" – trans-exclusionary radical feminists – with the suggestion that their views are inherently transphobic. This accusation seems unfounded. At the moment it is clear that intelligent, unprejudiced people disagree about this. So my position is simple: one side is wrong, we don't know for sure which, but that does not mean they are hateful or bigoted.

Rowling set off a Twitter-storm in which she was denounced as "going full Terf". She was accused of indicating that discrimination against a tweeter's trans daughter was "perfectly fine behaviour for an employee", of using her platform "to be cruel and exclusionary to one of the world's most vulnerable populations", of "defending racists, transphobes and abusers", and much more.

That is what inspired this deleted tweet:
Spot the difference:
"JK Rowling is dangerously wrong about sex and gender.
JK Rowling hates trans people & denies their right to exist.
If you believe the 1st please don't tweet the 2nd.
(And don't tell me I hate trans people for saying this. I absolutely do not.)"
Reading it now, it seems innocuous, unobjectionable. And yet, I did not post it. It was not simply that I did not want to become an object

Words do not only convey information, they can actually do things

of hate, too. I thought about how being drawn into the mire would affect my partner and the Royal Institute of Philosophy for which I have a part-time role as academic director. I had organised a debate for the RIP in which a so-called Terf had spoken. It stoked a Twitter-storm that in the end came to nothing, but we had to get in extra security for the event just in case.

My reasoning is completely understandable. And yet I worry it resulted in a form a self-censorship that added up to complicity. If so, I know I am not alone. Ever since I got drawn into the trans debate I've been asking every female philosopher I meet to explain to me what they make of it.

One or two have defended the anti-gender critical line, none to my satisfaction. The majority have said they stand with gender-critical feminists. But few say anything publicly. They don't want their students boycotting their lectures or calling for their dismissal. The price of solidarity is just too high for them. I'm deeply disturbed by the ease with which they and I convince ourselves that it's best to keep out of this one and let the battle be fought by the zealots alone.

By not speaking out, I feel complicit in the persecution of reasonable people who are putting forward a position on the trans issue disputed by opponents with louder voices.

The idea that we all have an obligation to speak out about any and every injustice is too strong. But when we silence ourselves to make our own lives easier, we surely are being cowards, allowing questionable views to go unquestioned and abandoning those braver than ourselves to fend for themselves. ⊗

Julian Baggini is an author, philosopher and part of Index on Censorship's editorial board

PICTURED: The hands of a migrant worker employed to work in a coca plantation in Colombia, picking the leaves that are used to make cocaine

CREDIT: Luis Robayo/Getty

IN FOCUS

Generations apart?

Index brought families together in China and Turkey to see if taboos or censorship had changed over three generations. **Karoline Kan** reports from China and **Kaya Genç** reports from Turkey. They chatted about Turkish freedom of speech in universities, and in China sex and relationships

49(01): 58/62 I DOI: 10.1177/0306422020917082

GENERATION XXX

Karoline Kan listens to a Chinese grandfather and granddaughter discuss marriage and sex from past to present

WANG SHOUKUI WAS born in 1945, in a village near the northern Chinese port of Tianjin, the eldest of seven children in a peasant family. It was the year the war ended with Japan and four years before the Chinese Communist Party won the civil war and founded the People's Republic of China.

Shoukui is a product of old and new China. He grew up with one "re-education" campaign after another – including the teaching of new ideas and customs on marriage and relationships, when the Communist Party made laws to ban forced marriage and announced that women should enjoy the same rights as men. He went to the best school in his hometown and became a lawyer. But he believed in "*mendanghudui*" – an old Chinese saying that suggests that the families of a couple should match each other in terms of socio-economic status – so he married a woman from a neighbouring village. The couple married two months after their first meeting. They moved to a nearby town and had two sons. She was illiterate, but she was a kind woman who did all the housework and took care of his parents and their children. The family was more important than love in marriage at that time, anyway. His wife died in 1994 from cancer, and Shoukui remarried the next year. He and his second wife are now living in Tianjin.

Wang Shuo is the daughter of Shoukui's elder son. Born in 1995, Shuo belongs to the generation of the youngest millennials. Like most Chinese people her age, she is an only child. She grew up listening to K-pop and watching The Big Bang Theory. She's never had a boyfriend and is open to remaining single and having no kids, which her parents and grandfather cannot understand. She is a graduate student, majoring in biology at a college in Tianjin. The topics of marriage and sex are not banned in China, but she and her friends face many obstacles in freely expressing themselves on these issues.

Q: What do you think has changed in terms of freedom of expression on issues of relationships, marriage and sex in China?

Shoukui: I am reluctant to say the changes are about "freedom". I think the changes are more about social customs, because most of the topics that people of my generation didn't talk [about] in public, but young people do today, were not banned by the government – just, culturally, people were not comfortable with them. For example, when we were young, couples never said "love" to each other. "Love" was not a word banned by the communists, [but] in that kind of society it would be awkward to say it. I still don't understand why people say it in public today. If you love somebody, you prove it by actions. The younger generation make relationships and marriage look like such a big deal, talking about it all the time. They should be only a small part in your life. It is important, but you don't need to share your feelings with others. But, sure, if you say the cultural, social changes bring more "freedoms" on talking about these, I agree.

Shuo: I think people are more open to talking about marriage and relationships today. Actually, my mother loves to talk with me about what kind of boyfriend or husband I should have in the future. I know in the past it was not common for unmarried women to discuss it – even with their close family members. Women were supposed to be ignorant about these kinds of things. However, now parents and teachers still don't teach their kids about sex. I think what has improved is the public awareness on topics like sexual harassment and domestic violence. Those topics used to be considered as too private [to be] public topics. But now they are public concerns.

Q: What are the disadvantages women face in relationships and marriage? Is there enough space for women to speak out if their rights are violated?

Shoukui: Because I worked as a lawyer in a local

I don't think women have enough space to speak out because we do not make the rules

LEFT (CLOCKWISE FROM TOP): A family dining on the Ma Cheo commune outside Shanghai, 1964; Women take a selfie in the Chinese city of Nanjing; Students in conversation at the University of Fine Arts, Istanbul, in 1973; Retired Turkish architect Doğan Tuna and his granddaughter Alexandra de Cramer

→ court, I met many cases when women tried to seek justice but didn't know anything about law, or they were afraid to face the consequences. Chinese men, even the uneducated, the poor, the ones who are in a less advanced position in many ways, enjoy much more than women with the same socio-economic background. Rural women my age dared not speak against their in-laws, and once they were married they no longer belonged to their own families. They moved away to an environment where they had no support network. Their husbands were their everything, so when they faced domestic violence they had nobody to help them. I think it has improved hugely now. Young women are more likely to go to court today than men. I think young women are more open-minded, like to learn, and are eager to protect their rights. Today, the court I used to work at receives more divorce cases proposed by wives than husbands.

Shuo: People keep saying young women of my generation enjoy as many rights as men, but it's only on paper. Society still expects different things from women. The prejudice is always that women are less reasonable than men, so when they face problems in a relationship or marriage society trusts them less and thinks they are exaggerating and emotional. Although they could find help from the law, from lawyers, court, police, what would they face afterwards? And is society really helping? For example, maternity leave is basically only given to women, but is that benefiting women? Probably not, but if you complain people will tell you women and men are different. They say giving women maternity leave is helping women. The same group of people probably would say in other circumstances that companies should hire men rather than women, also because of the "natural differences between the two genders" and "women need to take maternity leave". So, I don't think women have enough space to speak out because we do not make the rules.

Q: What are the differences between your own opinions on marriage and relationships and those of other generations in your family?

Shoukui: To me, the core value of marriage and relationships should be responsibility more than love. I grew up with the PRC. The communism value was important in every aspect of society, including marriage. We very much valued contributing to society. Marrying and having children at the right time was also a part of contributing to the country and your family. The government wants young people to settle down, which would help maintain social stability, while having children to continue the bloodline is being responsible to the family. In our time, to get married, you had to get approval from your boss, let

alone your parents. But at least I met my wife many times before we got married. She was introduced by a family relative. Our marriage was not arranged. It was different from the marriage of my parents, who were born in the 1920s. They got married as teenagers and their wedding day was the first day they met. I had never heard my parents complain about anything about marriage, although I know a lot was wrong. People their age didn't know an alternative way of living. They never thought about divorce.

My son's generation grew up watching a lot of Hong Kong and Taiwan films and TV shows, which were mostly about love and relationships. I didn't like them, and many old-fashioned people thought that pop culture polluted the minds of the mainlanders. But, of course, my generation's attitudes also changed as the culture and society changed. For example, I remarried in my late 40s when my wife died. I knew people were more tolerant to me than to my second wife, whose first husband also died. Men remarrying was always normal, but not for women, especially when they were no longer young. However, women of all ages today remarry and would get blessings from their families.

Rural women my age dared not speak against their in-laws

I know nothing about my two granddaughters' lives, but I hope they will get married. Marriage and children give people the meaning of life, especially when they get old.

Shuo: I don't know much about the love stories of my grandparents. I guess they are not really keen to talk about it anyway. In a Chinese family, people are shy about these topics. But I have heard a bit about my parents' marriage. My father went to a matchmaker two dozen times and he had been picky until he met my mother. Families on both sides thought they were old enough to get married even though they were in their early 20s. They were not forced, but clearly pressured. I asked them why they didn't fight back, and they said unless you wanted to split up with the one you dated, you would marry soon. It was in 1998. And in 1999, they had me. They fought a lot, but they were always pressured to stay together in the name of benefiting me. Also, they were afraid a different person wouldn't make much difference.

I probably won't have a stable boyfriend or marriage. My mother doesn't treat that idea seriously. I just don't see why not if I work and can support myself financially. The society is not friendly to unmarried women, but it will change.

Q: Have you paid any attention to LGBTQ issues and same-sex marriage?

Shoukui: What is LGBTQ? (An explanation follows.) These are just jokes from people who have too much time and nothing else to do. Why should abnormal topics take people's time and attention? Allowing same-sex marriage would encourage more abnormal things in this country. These ideas are harmful ideas from foreign countries after the Reform and Opening Up in 1978. Freedom of speech should have boundaries. Black is never white.

Shuo: I have gay and lesbian classmates in the university. It's still a sensitive topic. We wouldn't say bad things in front of them but, also, we wouldn't say in public we support same-sex marriage. I guess the Chinese campus environment is still quite conservative. I have never read anything in the classroom about homosexuality. I watched some good films, European and American, about gay love. You cannot find Chinese films or TV shows describing homosexual people as normal people. They would get censored quickly. The environment here is that homosexuality is wrong, and the schools and teachers don't want to talk about it.

Karoline Kan is a regular contributor to Index on Censorship. She is a journalist based in Beijing, China

EXAMINING TURKEY'S SCHOOL DAYS

In the second of our cross-generational interviews, a journalist and her architect grandfather explore the reduction of freedom in Turkish universities from the 1950s to today. Kaya Genç reports

DOĞAN TUNA, A retired Turkish architect and scholar, recalls the day Mustafa Kemal Atatürk, his country's secularist founder, died in 1938. Aged seven, he wept with his classmates and travelled to Dolmabahçe, the Istanbul palace where Atatürk took his last breath, to show his gratitude. "I went twice," he said. "We were brought up as Atatürk's followers."

Tuna came of age during the 1950s, a decade that saw Turkey experiment with multi-party democracy in the wake of Atatürk's modernising reforms. Tuna savoured Turkey's cosmopolitan new atmosphere where radical ideas could be freely debated.

"Our professors called from Bonn and Cologne. We could discuss anything with them! Our schools hosted debating societies which contributed greatly to freedom of expression [during] the 1950s. We'd go to meeting halls to watch law and political science students debate political subjects. Those were broadcast live on the radio. That was a healthy medium for debate and dialogue. Students would vote to decide who won the argument. We believed that a student who stayed silent in a university meant nothing. Universities are about universalism; with

silenced students who just complete their homework, what you actually have are vocational schools."

Tuna is talking about his university years with Alexandra de Cramer, his 31-year-old granddaughter. They are sitting in the living room of Tuna's house in the Aegean city of Izmir for an interview arranged by Index. Between 1992 and 1995, Tuna was the dean of a leading fine arts college in the city. His post allowed him to observe Turkey's declining academic freedom first-hand.

We believed that a student who stays silent in a university meant nothing

While studying political science during the 2000s, de Cramer found herself in an atmosphere of declining academic freedom. "I graduated from high school in 2006 when Turkish universities were starting to resemble the vocational schools you've described," she told her grandfather. "The system that provided those academic freedoms you cherished were, by then, over."

De Cramer asks her grandfather about the factors behind the academic freedoms of

→

the 1950s. "Firstly, there was no centralised control over universities," Tuna said. "The freedom of expression before the military coup in 1960 was so strong! Universities self-administered. Secondly, young people felt much freer. Political freedoms animated us." He recalls marching to Taksim Square with fellow students. "Teaching assistants marched alongside us. The police didn't intervene. They were there to protect us."

In the Turkey of de Cramer's youth, the kind of political student march Tuna describes would have been unthinkable. Instead, over the past half-decade, she anxiously watched crackdown after crackdown on Turkish scholars. Only last year, about 700 academics, mostly outspoken critics of Turkey's treatment of Armenians, Kurds and other political dissidents, were criminally charged, accused of supporting terror after they signed a petition calling for the resumption of a peace process.

De Cramer claims such authoritarian measures have created apathy among university students. "Turkey today doesn't allow its students to be cultured. A recent survey found that the first thing my generation would sell in Turkey would be their citizenship! The youth have had enough of this country."

Over the past half-decade, she anxiously watched crackdown after crackdown on Turkish scholars

Tuna contrasts this catastrophic state of affairs with the virtues of the "republican education system" he encountered half a century ago. "During my time, faculties were independent. Everything changed in 1982, with the foundation of the Council of Higher Education, which centralised all decision-making in Ankara." De Cramer asks whose idea that was. "Well, that brings us to the 1980 coup," he says, reminding her of the US support in that military takeover. "Thanks to those interventions, universities have become something else entirely."

But the 2010s came with an interest among Turkish scholars and students in breaking long-held taboos on subjects including the Armenian genocide, LGBTQ rights, feminism and the Kurdish question. This allowed de Cramer to learn about these issues before she moved to Beirut to cover the Arab Spring in 2011 for Turkish newspaper Milliyet. She then settled in London, joining Monocle magazine.

De Cramer sees a correlation between a lack of academic freedom and young people's unwillingness to continue living in Turkey. In a recent Arab Daily piece on Turkey's "lost generation", The Betrayal of Turkey's Youth, she pondered what her country, with a median age of 30, offered its university students.

"In the last 15 years, the number of unemployed university graduates has increased tenfold. Currently, 26% of university graduates are unable to find a job." Because of the clampdown on academic freedom, she noted, "it is little wonder that Turkey's finest brains have sought opportunities elsewhere".

As a retired educator, Tuna seems depressed about this state of affairs. To offer her a way out, he details the 1950s' equalitarian workplace culture that de Cramer's generation lacks. "We had high ethical standards; we saw little favouritism or nepotism. But after the coup in 1960, the Turkish military throttled this lenient atmosphere."

He also identifies a geopolitical shift as one reason behind the current lack of academic freedoms. "For my entry exam at Istanbul's prestigious Technical University, I wrote an essay on Viktor Kravchenko's I Chose Freedom – a Ukrainian-born Soviet defector's tale about oppression in his homeland. Turkey had close ties with Europe and the USA back then; my three-page essay won me a place at school." In contrast, today Turkish universities are increasingly run by professors whose ideas are echoed by the government's embrace of regimes such as those in Azerbaijan, China, Iran, Russia and Venezuela.

Tuna and de Cramer discuss unchanging attitudes against academic freedom between the 1950s and the 2010s, and the anti-intellectualism of Turkey's leaders stands out. "Prime Minister [Adnan] Menderes made a grave mistake," Tuna recalled, "when he mocked professors who criticised his rule by calling them 'scholars in cloaks' in the 1950s." De Cramer shouts: "It is the same intellectual-bashing we have in the 2020s!"

She describes how students can no longer express themselves at school. "Of course they can't. They don't have the platforms we've had," Tuna said. "And the taboos appear to have increased," his granddaughter interjects. Then she points to improvements: "I think taboos about female scholars partly disappeared for my generation. All girls my age go to college with aspirations for careers nowadays. I think that was different in your time."

When Tuna says that he "wouldn't like to grow up in today's Turkey because there is no future here", de Cramer lets out a little scream. "Granddad! What are people like me supposed to do, then?" Tuna considers the question for a moment. "Each has to find their own solution," he murmured, refusing to strike a note of optimism. But then he drops the name of Greta Thunberg as a potential symbol of hope for Turkish students. He wishes Turkish academies would allow local Gretas to emerge and question the system as diligently as she does, and he sees a parallel between Sweden's liberal education system and the Turkish education system of his youth.

"Nobody is outspoken like her these days," he said. "Only Greta has the guts. If she was my granddaughter, I'd kiss her on the forehead."

Kaya Genç is a contributing editor at Index on Censorship. He is based in Istanbul

Crossing the line

Cocaine use is soaring in Colombia, and so is the power of the cartels to stop journalists working.
Stephen Woodman reports

49(01): 63/65 I DOI: 10.1177/0306422020917083

EDUARDO MANZANO CAN recite the threatening text messages from memory. "We have you on our hit list. You are a military target and we will not rest until you die," the first message began.

Manzano received the threats after reporting on criminal gangs stealing electricity for their drug crops in south-west Colombia. After assessing his case, the government offered him a bodyguard, a bulletproof vest and a panic button.

He saw those measures as inappropriate and told Index: "I am constantly challenging the authorities. Those same authorities can't guard me."

Each year, the United Nations prepares new campaigns, reports and data to promote the war on drugs ahead of the International Day against Drug Abuse and Illicit Trafficking on 26 June.

But the UN's statistics show drug use is soaring, fuelling black market criminality that creates a climate of fear in countries such as Colombia, where illicit cultivation is rife.

Empowered Colombian criminals are increasingly targeting journalists and social activists. Mexican drug cartels have also expanded their role in the country and are aggressively silencing those standing in the way of their smuggling networks.

To combat this crisis, Colombia's government has allocated more than £200m ($253.7m) to protect journalists and activists in 2020. But experts say drug gangs now have the power to overwhelm, and even corrupt, the very institutions charged with protecting freedom of expression.

At least five reporters in the south-western Cauca province received death threats last year. The messages were signed by the Western Joint Command of the Sixth Front, an obscure group of dissidents that once belonged to the now-disarmed Revolutionary Armed Forces of Colombia, or Farc. The threats signalled the start of a campaign of intimidation that has forced three of the five journalists, including Manzano, to flee the country.

South-west Colombia is a key hub for drug cultivation, and few places in the world are more closely tied to the latest trends in global drug markets.

The 2019 UN World Drug Report indicates that more people than ever are smoking marijuana around the world, in line with an estimated rise in global supply.

According to the UN, cocaine use is also increasing, and manufacture of the drug reached an all-time high in 2017, the most recent year for which estimates are available. Colombia drove this upward trend, producing an estimated 70% of the total.

Preliminary data from the next World Drug Report, to be released in June, points to a tiny decline in Colombian coca cultivation in 2018. However, it was still the second highest year for production on record.

Drug crops have boomed in the wake of the historic peace deal Colombia signed with the leftist Farc guerrillas in 2016. The agreement

---

Drug gangs now have the power to overwhelm, and even corrupt, the very institutions charged with protecting freedom of expression

ABOVE: Police stand guard over packages of cocaine that were about to be illegally shipped to the Netherlands

– which ended 52 years of bloody conflict – included a subsidy scheme for coca farmers who switched to growing legal crops.

But the government has faltered in its commitments. According to the UN, fewer than half the families enrolled in the programme have received the full promised payment. In the Cauca province, nearly 30% of families have received nothing in return for volunteering to destroy their coca crops.

Meanwhile, armed groups are competing for the country's lucrative drug fields.

"The restructuring of powers [in Cauca] means it has become a zone of both major journalistic interest and great censorship," said Luisa Fernanda Isaza, of Colombia's Foundation for Press Freedom (Flip), a non-governmental body.

Nearly 40% of Cauca's population lives in an area without a local media outlet, and security concerns are a key factor behind that

trend. Last year, Flip documented 19 acts of aggression against the press in Cauca alone. Those included threats and harassment, physical attacks, property damage, illegal detentions and obstruction of journalistic work.

Community leaders, politicians and activists faced even greater violence. In September last year, assailants opened fire on a car carrying mayoral candidate Karina García before setting the vehicle alight. García, her mother and four others died in the attack.

In October, five members of an indigenous defence force were massacred on a routine patrol of one of Cauca's native communities. State authorities blamed Farc dissidents for the killings.

These were part of a wave of attacks that swept the country. The Institute of Studies for Development and Peace (Indepaz), a Colombian NGO, counts 756 killings of defenders between the signing of the peace deal in November 2016 and January this year.

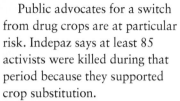

Public advocates for a switch from drug crops are at particular risk. Indepaz says at least 85 activists were killed during that period because they supported crop substitution.

Colombia's president, Iván Duque, recently told the national newspaper El Tiempo that Mexico's Sinaloa Cartel had played a role in his country's criminal landscape for many years.

Historically, Mexican criminals were limited to distribution, trafficking drugs to the North American and European markets. But wealthy Mexican cartels are now taking a direct role in drug production to iron out potential supply chain problems, and Colombia's government has documented a sharp increase in Mexicans participating in illegal activities within Colombia since 2014.

Many observers living near Colombia's coca and marijuana fields draw a link between the arrival of Mexican criminals and rising instability.

"Colombian armed groups used to bring the drugs to strategic points," said one journalist, who asked not to be named. "Now the Mexicans have come here and sparked more violence."

Last year, the Indigenous Regional Council of Cauca raised the alert about a statement published under the insignia of the New Generation Sinaloa Cartel on social media. The message warned indigenous defenders they would "slaughter them like animals" if their operations were disrupted.

In a statement published last November, Flip also tied the recent campaign of intimidation against journalists to their "denouncing the presence of Mexican cartels, allied with Farc dissidents in the region".

Alexander Cárdenas, a cameraman who worked alongside Manzano at Caracol Television, was one of the five media workers who received death threats last year.

Threatening journalists, burning candidates, we've not seen this before

In July, a group of men with Mexican accents approached Cárdenas in northern Cauca. The men ordered him to stop filming and leave. Despite their threats, he published the report, an action he sees as a catalyst for the aggression that began the following month.

"I have been going to northern Cauca for 23 years," he told Index. "I have seen people die in conflicts. I've seen soldiers die. But no one has ever told us we can't be there… Threatening journalists, burning candidates, we've not seen this before."

Cárdenas changed his address three times to avoid the aggressors. He was staying at his sister's house when two men rang the doorbell and demanded to know his whereabouts. Cárdenas escaped through the back door and left the country two days later.

Like Manzano, Cárdenas was forced into exile despite receiving attention from Colombia's National Protection Unit. This federal agency manages the safeguarding of more than 8,000 activists, politicians and journalists, among others.

An official assessment concluded both Manzano and Cárdenas were at extraordinary risk. However, police failed to provide the routine patrols promised as part of the security schemes.

But those inconsistencies were less alarming than the discovery made just weeks later, when a government raid on the offices of the agency revealed at least one of its officials had collected security data and sold it to criminals.

Cárdenas, who had already left the country when the news broke, asked: "How can those who are supposed to protect you sell your private information to those who want to kill you?" ⊗

Stephen Woodman *is Index's contributing editor in Mexico*

A slap in the face

The Di Nicola bill, due to be passed into law this summer, should reduce vexatious lawsuits against Italian journalists. **Alessio Perrone** talks to those who have fought off attempts to stop them reporting

49(01): 66/68 I DOI: 10.1177/0306422020917084

FEDERICA ANGELI TOOK to social media to celebrate being found not guilty in a defamation case for the 111th time in her career.

"I felt a very strong sense of tiredness," the La Repubblica reporter told Index. "You never get used to being sued – each time is a blow to the heart, a hassle and a waste of your time."

After having to confront 126 lawsuits – 15 are still ongoing – she says that she has developed a "phobia". "Now, almost every article I write is met with a nearly automatic lawsuit," she said.

Italy has failed to curb vexatious lawsuits, also known as Slapps (Strategic Lawsuits Against Public Participation). These differ from "simple" defamation lawsuits because they set out with little or no chance of success, ask a disproportionate amount for damages and primarily aim to silence critics.

In 2016, a bill came close to reforming the code of civil procedure, introducing penalties for vexatious lawsuits and generating optimism among journalists and free speech NGOs. But then it stalled in parliament and was killed.

But a new bill, named after Primo Di Nicola, the journalist-turned-MP who promoted it, is generating hope. Like its predecessors, it would deter suitors by introducing sanctions of up to 50% of the damages they asked for if their lawsuit was ruled to be vexatious. The bill was presented in 2018, and stalled in parliament for months like the other bills. But in late 2019, the text was tabled for discussion at the Senate and could be approved as soon as June 2020.

For some, it represented a glimmer of hope and a call to arms. "If the [Di Nicola] bill should again get bogged down in parliament, we will have to gather all reporters in parliament to request that politicians stop just expressing solidarity for journalists – and legislate instead," said Giuseppe Giulietti, the president of the National Federation of the Italian Press.

Angeli's energies have been drained to the extent that sometimes she feels tempted to settle the remaining lawsuits, giving up the fight even though she believes she is innocent – although it is a temptation that she would never allow herself to give in to.

Crucially, her feelings are not a lesson on the dangers of shoddy reporting. Angeli's work took down members of the mafia and has won her a plethora of awards. After she and her family were forced to live under police protection in 2013, her life was found so inspiring it was turned into a film.

Her case illustrates how vexatious defamation lawsuits are often used to intimidate journalists and pressure them to self-censor. For many facing steep legal fees and lengthy trials, dropping an investigation is not an act of surrender, but self-preservation.

You never get used to being sued – each time is a blow to the heart, a hassle and a waste of your time

"If someone is backed by a strong publisher, they can resist," said Giulietti. "But if they are freelancers, or small newspapers, they'll make a reflection before carrying on with their work."

After all, if lawsuits have managed to wear down someone as experienced and accomplished as Angeli, who is backed by a strong publisher, what happens to the others?

While not exclusive to Italy, vexatious defamation lawsuits have proliferated in the country to the point that Carlo Verna, president of the Order of Journalists, has called them a "democratic emergency". According to the most recent analysis by Ossigeno per l'Informazione, an Italian observatory on

threats to journalists, almost 70% of the 9,000-plus lawsuits that courts examined in 2016 never went to trial.

In part, this is because – unlike in other countries – there are virtually no drawbacks to suing for defamation in Italy. For example, laws fail to punish those who file spurious suits and defendants can be bound to pay legal fees even if they are not found guilty, making defendants easy targets and easy victims.

Politicians are often the perpetrators of Slapps in Italy, according to Paola Rosà, who – together with colleague Claudia Pierobon and the Balkan and Caucasus Observatory – has studied the problem for the European

ABOVE: A woman marches on the streets of Rome at a protest to demand freedom of the press in May, 2019

If you put your hands on big news about a public figure with the tendency to sue, you'll think twice. I have never stopped, but many give up because they fear consequences that they can't afford

→ Centre for Press and Media Freedom.

"One lawsuit is enough to ruin your life," she said. "It means wasting time, [needing] money, finding a lawyer, dealing with mail and paperwork.

"Journalists won't be so sure to carry on with their work if they fear they might have to sell their home to pay legal fees," she added. "It's not just psychological intimidation, it disrupts a journalist's daily life."

For many, the financial threat of legal fees hits the hardest.

"If you face this uncertainty – you never know how it ends with the law – then you don't take risks, you don't invest," said Luca Muzzioli, editor of Volleyball.it. Muzzioli carried on working as he fought a €2 million claim by politician Mauro Fabris, national president of the Women's Volleyball League Serie A, between 2009 and 2015 and is now facing the threat of a new lawsuit by a club president, among other forms of intimidation. As an entrepreneur and publisher who often relies only on his own forces to keep the site going, he explains that even the relatively tiny sum of legal fees can scare a small publisher away from critical reporting, although he stresses it hasn't in his case.

"If you know you could end up needing €10,000 for legal fees, would you use the money to hire a contributor, travel to the world cup or expand the site?" he said.

To carry on reporting fearlessly under the constant threat of litigation requires determination, courage and "recklessness", a pressure that few can endure, says Antonella Napoli, editor-in-chief of Focus on Africa and board member of free-speech watchdog Articolo 21.

Like Angeli, she has also been at the centre of a case demonstrating the grotesque levels of intimidation that Slapps can reach in Italy. Napoli has faced only one Slapp case in her career so far, but it is one that has dragged on for a whopping 22 years.

It started in 1998 when she reported on a politician's misappropriation of public funds. She based her report on official documents and police records, but the politician decided to cite her for damages anyway. When he died, his family picked up the fight.

"You feel gagged, tied, especially if you are a freelance journalist," she said. "If you get your hands on big news about a public figure with the tendency to sue, you'll think twice. I have never stopped, but many give up because they fear consequences that they can't afford."

Some have taken the news of the change in the law with a pinch of salt, conscious of the many botched attempts over the last 20 years, and the situation feels like another uphill battle sending ripples of a familiar sense of tiredness.

"I don't believe in reform anymore," said a disillusioned Angeli. "If politicians are the top perpetrators, why would anyone commit to something that could backfire against them?" ⊗

__Alessio Perrone__ is an Italian journalist, who reports regularly for Index on Censorship

LEGAL THREATS TO JOURNALISTS: CALL FOR CONTRIBUTIONS

Index on Censorship has recently launched a year-long research and policy project on vexatious law suits (Slapps), looking at their impact across Europe. It will include interviews with investigative journalists and lawyers. If you are a journalist and would be willing to be interviewed for the research, please email: **jessica@indexoncensorship.org**

Con (census)

As countries look to postpone censuses, **Jessica Ní Mhainín** looks at how data on LGBTQ people is also being left out

49(01): 69/71 | DOI: 10.1177/0306422020917086

KAREEM CHEHAYEB IS frequently met with a wall of questions when he tries to access government-sourced information in his native Lebanon.

"They say, 'Why do you want this information? Is this your concern? Why are you writing about this? Are you trying to spin it in a negative way?" said Chehayeb, a Beirut-based investigative journalist. Even if he does receive the requested information, he doesn't necessarily feel he can trust it.

"They sometimes pick out selective supplementary information to boost things up a bit," he said.

Lebanon hasn't carried out a census since 1932, and Chehayeb feels particularly unable to trust data on the population.

"It's a huge problem, especially if you're doing a human-centred piece or an economic piece, right?" he said. "How can you gauge the Lebanese labour force? How can you really get an idea of what the unemployment rate is in Lebanon?

"I always try to look at other information to try to triangulate with what I'm given." He does so by looking at data from international organisations, such as the UN, and from local institutions working on the ground.

This is an important year, with several countries, including the USA and Russia, due to hold their national censuses. Knowing that you are getting the right information is crucial but,

as Chehayeb attests, it's not always easy.

The original censor was a Roman magistrate tasked with conducting the census (along with overseeing public manners and morals). Today, a census is widely viewed as an apolitical process that merely seeks to count all the residents of a given territory. But censuses and population surveys can be as political as they are scientific: leaders have a vested interest in how many people respond and how people define themselves. As such, population data is vulnerable to political manipulation.

Some leaders may seek to put off censuses for fear that controversial results might be politically damaging. In divided societies such as Lebanon, officially acknowledging the demographic growth of one community (Christian, Shia, Sunni) over another could also provoke civil unrest. Nevertheless, it is important for accurate population data to be collected and for the results to be made available.

"It's in the public interest," said Laurence Cooley, a political scientist at the University of Birmingham in the UK, whose research investigates the politics of the census. "It's also about generating data on socio-economic conditions, which is important for planning purposes."

More and more countries, the UK among them, are considering replacing the census with administrative data and large-scale population surveys. But according to Jaime Nadal of the United Nations Population Fund, while the use of big data is very practical, it does not replace a census. Unless countries have a compulsory population register, "the only way to make visible [that which is] invisible is collecting information through a census".

Governments almost always publish census data lest they be seen as having something to hide, although the Soviet Union's action in 1937 showed that withholding such data happens.

"The organisers [of the census] were arrested and shot," explained Dominique Arel, →

The organisers [of the census] were arrested and shot

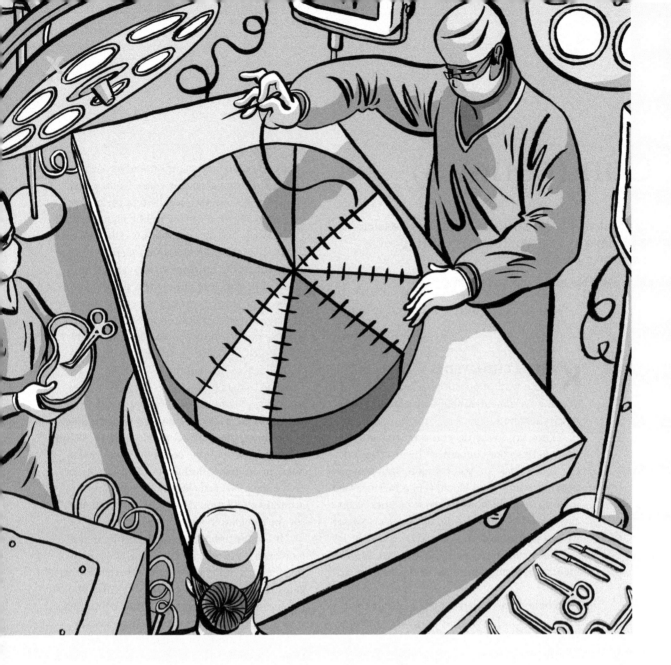

CREDIT: Dom McKenzie/Ikon

chair of Ukrainian studies at the University of Ottawa. Soviet leader Joseph Stalin did not like the results of the census because they showed that the overall population had not grown as he expected.

Arel said: "[1937] was the year of the great purges, when almost a million people were shot on fabricated charges and many more were sent to the gulag." The decline in population numbers could also be attributed to the 1932-33 famine, which killed millions of people, even though its existence was denied by the authorities.

A fake census was conducted in 1939 and the falsified results were subsequently released. The results from 1937 remained state secrets until the fall of the Soviet Union.

Nowadays, it is more common for countries to exclude specific communities from population data. On the one hand, as societies become increasingly complex and diverse, groups can be excluded by default when governments don't improve their methodologies and don't increase census budgets. People can be omitted by design, on the other hand, when governments discriminate against certain groups. During Burma's 2014 census, enumerators refused to count the country's Rohingya Muslim population, which at the time – two years before the beginning of the genocide – amounted to about 1.3 million people.

In the USA, where the 2020 census had been scheduled for 1 April, default and design have conspired to see the exclusion of LGBTQ

The gender of couples that indicated they were in same-sex couples was recoded (as if to correct an error)

communities from population data. Until the 1990 census, the gender of couples that indicated they were in same-sex couples was recoded (as if to correct an error) so that data files showed a different-sex couple. In 1980, more than three million people had their sex chosen by a computer. The Census Bureau no longer recodes responses, but the discrimination continues.

According to organisations working to advance LGBTQ rights, the Donald Trump administration has tried to diminish data that is being collected on those communities.

"They're stopping data collection on communities that [the Trump administration doesn't] want a public narrative to exist for, and they're creating the data that will support narratives they want to tell," said Meghan Maury, of the National LGBT Task Force.

At the same time, citizenship questions have, she said, been added to "a tonne of criminal justice surveys" in what appears to be an effort to drum up data linking immigrants to crime. "We're seeing this administration playing politics with science and trying to do harm to our long-term ability to advocate for communities of colour and for LGBTQ folks, by making sure that there's not the data we need to move those policy points forward."

Aaron Tax, of Sage USA, an organisation dedicated to advocating for older LGBTQ people, gives the example of the Trump administration's efforts to edit a national survey of elderly Americans that measures the efficiency of government programmes aimed at meeting their needs.

"The one and only question in this more than a 100-page survey that the Trump administration tried to remove was the LGBT demographic question," he said. While a question addressing the "LGB" demographic has since been put back in, efforts to reinclude a transgender question have been unsuccessful.

"I think it speaks to a larger issue that we see across this administration in trying to erase

the existence of LGBT people at large in all sorts of data collection instruments, including the census."

Hungary's far-right government is also alleged to have changed the metrics by which it measures population data, specifically around unemployment and poverty. According to data journalist Attila Bátorfy, of investigative news site Atlatszo.hu, domestic data places Hungary among the countries with the lowest unemployment rate in the EU. "But if we count [according to] the original EU standard, Hungary has the second highest unemployment rate in the EU."

Bátorfy is increasingly mistrustful of the information provided by the government. "Sometimes you have a feeling that what you get or what is publicly available is not reliable or is manipulated."

He says that although the authorities usually fulfil their obligations under freedom of information laws, the data is often full of errors and inconsistencies, and is sometimes unreadable.

Bátorfy uses data from Eurostat or the World Bank to compensate for the lack of reliable government information. "International conventions and contracts obligate governments to provide data according to international standards; the methodology, sample, definitions should be the same, or at least comparable," he said.

"From 1948 to 1990, state institutions and agencies published mostly false information on society, but everyone knew that they were manipulating data and graphics in the service of communist propaganda. I never thought that, as a journalist and academic, I would face this problem again."

Jessica Ní Mhainín is policy research and advocacy officer at Index on Censorship

THE DOCUMENTARY BOLSONARO DOESN'T WANT MADE

Transversais, a Brazilian documentary
TV series about transgender people,
has yet to be made as a result of
President Jair Bolsonaro cancelling
its financing. Here, for the first time,
we publish excerpts from its pitch

~

October 24, 2018

Draft #5

(Copyright 2020)

49(01): 72/74 | DOI: 10.1177/0306422020917087

Why it should be commissioned

To document in a TV series the story of five transgender people in the process of changing their bodies to match their gender identity is, first of all, to give voice to an urgent debate in our society. A population that is still unknown to most, the trans community is viewed with strangeness and distrust, even amongst members of the gay and lesbian community.

Casting a spotlight on such a niche theme is of fundamental importance for the establishment, and the exercise, of full rights for these people. Only from the deconstruction of stereotypes and from a real representation of their daily lives and dramas will we be able to envision the real inclusion of these people. And this is what Transversais proposes.

With Transversais, we will approach this largely unknown universe. But our guiding approach will not be that of strangeness or that of the attractions of "freak shows" commonly directed at them. Our approach will start from the opposite bias. We will show that trans people lead a normal life, with regular ambitions and joys like anyone else: feeling comfortable in front of the mirror, being happy in love, being respected at work, being able to use public bathrooms without fear of violence, being close to the family.

We will monitor their daily lives, their personal relationships, their family tensions, their life goals. We will investigate their memories, traumas, decisive moments, joy, pride. The protagonist will not be that of just transgender but actually of the person they are in all aspects. At the same time, we will research the construction of this public idea of transgender and the physical transformation they must undergo. We will bring to the foreground this population that usually lives on the margins. We will shed light on them, making the invisible notable and giving a voice to the silenced.

Who it will target

The target audience of this documentary series is young people and adults, of both sexes and all social classes, interested in discussions around current affairs and society, such as the perception of the other, the sense of otherness, gender identity, →

"EACH DAY IS GETTING HARDER"

RACHAEL JOLLEY talks to film director Émerson Maranhão about how his TV show on transgender people has been censored by Brazil's president

DOCUMENTARY DIRECTOR ÉMERSON Maranhão says he considers the censorship of his TV series Transversais, about the lives of transgender people in Brazil, a landmark in terms of the political direction of the current government.

"It was the first time that the president has acted explicitly to prevent the production of cultural products that he considers 'inadequate'," he said.

President Jair Bolsonaro has removed nearly $17 million of funding for the film industry. At the same time this happened, says Maranhão, censorship of other arts projects was announced, theatrical shows were closed down, exhibitions were censored and book launches at public universities were cancelled.

"All these artistic events had themes at odds with the thinking of the current government," he said. The most obvious area of conflict was respect for the "traditional family" and the "Christian faith", a favourite policy area of the ultra-conservative and evangelical voters who support the president.

The feeling we have is that this government tests the strength of our democracy all the time, he said. "When

ABOVE: The director Émerson Maranhão, whose film about trans people has been cancelled in Brazil

→ civil rights and prejudice. It is also an audience interested in knowing good stories and getting in touch with a world that, although most of the time seems invisible, actually lives alongside us. As one of the aims of this work is to demystify transgender, which is still obscure for the majority of the population, the broader its scope the greater its effectiveness. Therefore, we want it to be accessible to large numbers of viewers.

Who it will feature: Kaio Lemos

Transgender man. Lemos, 38 years old, is an academic researcher and has a bachelor's degree in humanities. The youngest of five children from his parents' first marriage, he was raised by an evangelical mother as a girl. To this day, his mother does not accept his gender status. He is a trans activist, and in 2017 he founded a shelter to help transsexual people in vulnerable situations. Fourteen people have so far been sheltered. The house is maintained thanks to donations.

What it will cover: Episode 4

Pacatuba, Ceará. Samilla Marques made adversity the driving force for her personal revolution. Born and raised in an evangelical family, she faced challenges from everyone when she decided to become a woman. She left home, became a hairdresser, entered university and, slowly, gained the respect of those who had judged her. Through her own merits, she held important public positions and was a pioneer in the fight for sexual diversity and the rights of trans people in Ceará. Today, she returns to the church where she was raised and takes her parents to Sunday services. She is also her nephews' favourite aunt. ⊗

the reaction of the population and the media is great, [Bolsonaro] backs off and says that everything was just a misunderstanding; otherwise, it advances and rises another step in the stifling of democratic principles.

"I think that each day is getting harder and the trend is getting worse. There is a great polarisation in Brazil today – a polarisation that reaches the verge of irrationality. And this polarisation is part of the continuous stimulus to what they call 'cultural war' – that is, the systematic disqualification of any cultural product that does not reflect the world view of a certain group."

Today, there is a great tug-of-war over Brazil's history. And the right, which is now in power, pays special attention to this. Maranhão says this cultural war relies on historical revisionism. It argues, for instance, that Nazism was a left-wing political movement, that African slavery was voluntary, that the Earth is flat, or that there was no torture during the military dictatorship in Brazil. In fact, they assert that there was no "dictatorship" but simply a "military regime".

"It is strategic for these politicians on the extreme right that their versions are dominant and unquestionable. Any attempt at questioning their values is quashed," said Maranhão.

Meanwhile, there are ongoing attacks on the documentary The Edge of Democracy by director Petra Costa. The film, which was nominated for an Oscar for Best Documentary, argues that former president Dilma Rousseff was overthrown by a parliamentary coup. The news of the nomination was scorned by the government, which accused the director of being "anti-Brazil".

The Transversais series competed in a public tender for funding and was announced as a finalist in the Projects on Gender Diversity category in May 2019. In August, the president announced he was to cancel some of the funding. The first on the list was Transversais, and the cancellation of three other projects on sexuality and gender diversity were also announced.

Maranhão appealed to the courts, which ruled in his favour. The government appealed but lost. At the end of January 2020, the result of the public tender was finally announced. To the shock of no one, none of the four projects whose censorship had previously been announced by Bolsonaro was included.

Efforts are currently being made to obtain the minutes of the judging committee's meetings made public. Maranhão wants to be sure of what really happened and to know if there was an order for those projects to be excluded.

Rachael Jolley is the editor of Index

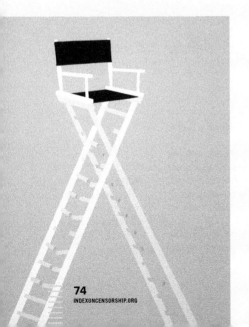

Queer erasure

In a magazine exclusive, **April Anderson** and **Andy Lee Roth** reveal original research showing how search engines are filtering out pro-LGBTQ stories and amplifying homophobic voices

49(01): 75/77 I DOI: 10.1177/0306422020917088

FROM CENSORING CONTENT as "ob-jectionable" to blacklisting keywords and restricting users' advertising revenue, major media platforms are filtering online speech in ways that marginalise and stigmatise LGBTQ communities, as we reveal in research carried out exclusively for Index.

The same mechanisms that block LGBTQ-themed hashtags on Instagram or demonetise LGBTQ channels on YouTube, for example, also often permit – or even promote – anti-LGBTQ content.

Our research also showed that Google News was one of the worst offenders. We conducted a study of the news aggregator from 3 to 7 February 2020, using "LGBT" and related search terms. In that period we found that Google News consistently provided a prominent platform for evangelical Christian and far-right perspectives on LGBTQ issues.

On 6 February, for example, Google News featured an article from the Christian Post asserting that Disney and other Hollywood studios were "capitulating to character quotas" and "virtue signalling to the loud and influential LGBT lobby". The following day, it highlighted an article by Tony Perkins, president of the arch-conservative Family Research Council, decrying an "LGBT agenda" that rejected "biblical teaching on sex and marriage". Perkins' organisation has been designated a hate group by the Southern Poverty Law Centre because of its record of defaming gays and lesbians "based on discredited research and junk science".

Overall, 46% of the LGBTQ stories spotlighted by Google News in our research derived from conservative news outlets, including 32% from conservative Christian sources. By contrast, only 4% of LGBTQ stories featured by Google News – one from Mother Jones on former Democrat presidential contender Pete Buttigieg and another from Human Rights Watch about health policies in Tanzania – originated from progressive outlets. Despite an abundance of excellent news organisations dedicated to reporting LGBTQ issues, Google News featured none during the week studied. We asked Google for comments on the research, but it did not respond.

Our findings corroborate a study of Google News from September 2019 by Matt Tracy for Gay City News. Tracy conducted a systematic study of Google News's anti-LGBTQ bias after noticing how often in the course of his work the engine returned "inflammatory, bigoted content" that seemed at odds with general attitudes on LGBTQ topics.

Our study compared the Google's news aggregator to another search engine. Searching the same terms in the same week using the news service of DuckDuckGo produced contrasting results. Only 6% of DuckDuckGo's LGBTQ articles derived from conservative, religious or more politically biased sources. Instead, it more frequently featured mainstream US news sources (56%) or international news sources (13%).

Google's selection algorithms for its news

Despite an abundance of excellent news organisations dedicated to reporting LGBTQ issues, Google News featured none

aggregator are unavailable for public scrutiny beyond the general terms in which they are described in the company's support portal and in interviews given by its executives. This makes it impossible to judge whether the prominence of anti-LGBTQ stories is due to in-built bias, skilful search engine optimisation by conservatives with homophobic agendas, or other factors.

A pending lawsuit filed in California in 2019 by LGBTQ content creators could force Google to make its powerful algorithms available for scrutiny. The class action complaint asserts that YouTube, the premier video sharing platform, and Google, its parent company, act as censors, regulating online content for their own gain.

The lawsuit contends that YouTube restricts LGBTQ content creators' access on the basis of their sexual orientation or gender identity. It identifies a "tool kit" of practices YouTube has used to do this, including content blocking, advertising restrictions and channel demonetisation. The complaint further alleges that YouTube promotes anti-LGBTQ content by playing anti-LGBTQ advertisements before LGBTQ videos and by permitting unmoderated hateful comments on LGBTQ videos.

According to the plaintiffs' lawyer, Peter Obstler, in addition to forcing YouTube to make its proprietary algorithms available for review, a ruling in his clients' favour could reveal if YouTube suppresses third-party content in order to reap greater profits by promoting its own content.

Despite efforts by Google/YouTube to dismiss the case, a federal hearing was scheduled for this spring. However, this may be postponed, because the US Department of Justice has informed the plaintiffs that the solicitor general will review Google/YouTube's claim to immunity under Section 230 of the 1996 Communications Decency Act. This constitutional issue, and the solicitor general's involvement, suggest that the case may ultimately be decided by the Supreme Court.

As that lawsuit progresses through US courts, advertisers around the world continue to use keyword blacklists that automatically flag terms deemed to be profit-threatening. In order to promote "brand safety", about 95% of advertisers now use these, according to Jonathan Marciano, director of communications at CHEQ, an advertising verification company.

A September 2019 study conducted by CHEQ found that keyword blacklists, which include terms such as "bisexual" and "same-sex marriage", demonetise up to 73% of neutral or positive content on LGBTQ news outlets such as The Advocate and PinkNews. Lost advertising revenues may have also contributed to the closure of LGBTQ news outlets including The Pool and INTO.

The advertising industry's lack of understanding regarding the impact of keyword blacklists will likely lead to what Marciano described as "a slower death" for additional independent news outlets, further shrinking public access to reliable queer-focused resources online.

Sealow, a YouTuber whose research has identified more than 16,000 keywords used to demonetise YouTube channels, argues that researchers need more direct access to the systems used by platforms such as YouTube to

When Tumblr responded to changes in US law by removing all content it defined as "adult" … the decision didn't just affect queer communities in the United States

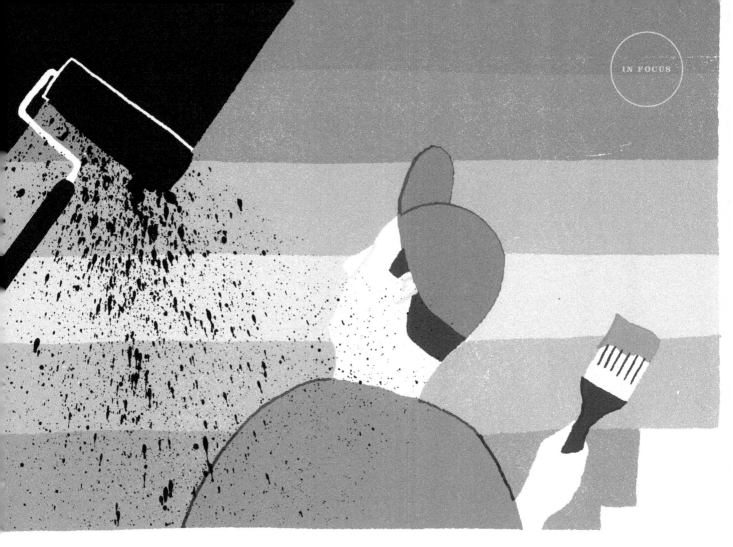

ensure that those systems function without any discriminatory behaviour.

Due to these platforms' global reach, this algorithmic censorship "applies across national boundaries", according to Patrick Keilty, a University of Toronto professor who researches the politics of digital infrastructures. For example, in December 2018, when Tumblr responded to changes in US law by removing all content it defined as "adult", Keilty observed that the decision didn't just affect queer communities in the United States. Those in Mexico, Canada, Germany, the Philippines and elsewhere also felt its impact.

Afsaneh Rigot, a research fellow at Harvard's Berkman Klein Centre, contends that everyday online tools, including group chat services and online dating apps, should be designed with "at-risk marginalised communities in mind" because doing so results in features and protections for all groups.

Recent studies, including Virginia Eubanks'

book Automating Inequality and Safiya Umoji Noble's Algorithms of Oppression, have raised public awareness and informed policy debate about how artificial intelligence can reflect and reinforce racist practices. The scope and complexity of content-blocking preclude any single, simple solution to the marginalisation of queer communities online. However, increasingly, algorithm-driven censorship is stifling LGBTQ freedom of expression and amplifying anti-LGBTQ animus, and urgently needs attention. ⊗

April Anderson is a librarian at Macalester College, Minnesota, and *Andy Lee Roth* is associate director of Project Censored, a media watchdog that promotes independent investigative journalism. Anderson and Roth co-authored Stonewalled: Establishment Media's Silence on the Trump Administration's Crusade against LGBTQ People

ORCE
RNESTO
OMERO
ACTOR

ALICIA
PALANCO
ACTRIZ

RAU
IGLE
ACT

A BI
GLD R
ACTO

MAIN: Protesters march through the streets of Buenos Aires, Argentina in 2018 for the Day of Remembrance for Truth and Justice. The national holiday commemorates the victims of the Dirty War of 1976 to 1983, during which thousands of people were disappeared

78
INDEXONCENSORSHIP.ORG

teatro x la identidad

CREDIT: Nicholas Tinelli/Alamy

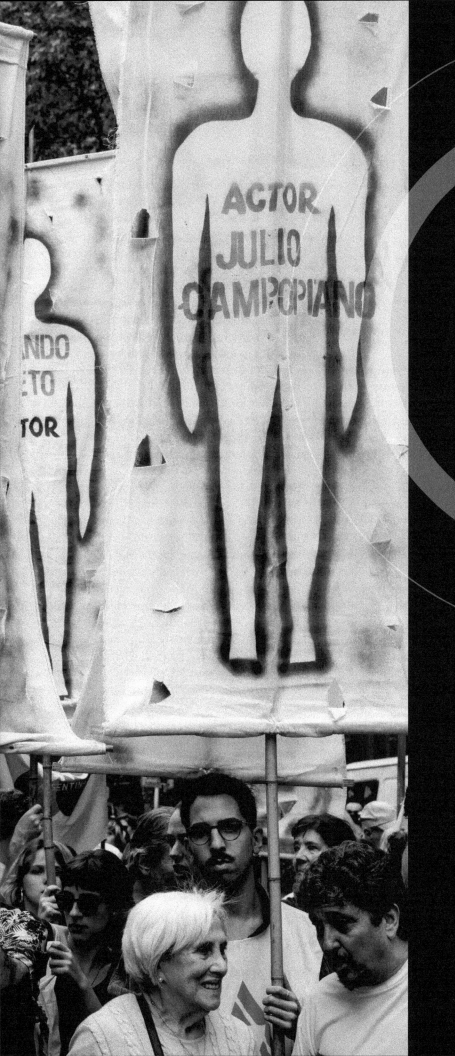

CULTURE

Up in smoke

The son of disappeared parents, Argentine writer **Félix Bruzzone** tells **Irene Caselli** about his grief and writing about the dictatorship

49(01): 80/85 I DOI: 10.1177/0306422020917089

IT IS A political and yet deeply personal event that marks the life and literary work of Argentinean writer Félix Bruzzone. In March 1976, soon after the military junta took power, Félix Roque Giménez, Bruzzone's father, was "disappeared". His mother, Marcela Bruzzone Moretti, was pregnant. Bruzzone was born in August and his mother was disappeared in November, when he was just three months old. It is with these autobiographical details that the short story Smoking Under Water (Fumar bajo del agua) begins – translated into English for the first time here.

The story's main character doesn't explain what happened to his parents. This is partly because the verb "to disappear" in Argentina is linked automatically to the actions of the dictatorship. But it is also because Bruzzone himself does not know yet what happened to his parents, as their bodies have never been recovered. They were left-wing militants who got caught in the military regime's masterplan to crush opponents, which resulted in the murder and disappearance of some 30,000 people.

Smoking Under Water is part of 76, a collection of short stories that deal with the dictatorship. Written in 2008, it was the first book published by the award-winning writer, who has been named one of the most important writers from Argentina by Clarín, the largest newspaper in the country.

"I had to deal with this trauma in order to fully dedicate myself to literature," Bruzzone told Index. "I had to do it explicitly in my writing before I could move away from it."

The ability to fictionalise part of his biography gave him a sense of freedom. Despite the political nature of the story's subject, there is nothing sacred about the way the story is told. On the contrary: the story veers away from real-life events and is irreverent. For example, the main character's loving grandmother, who had raised him, dies of a massive heart attack because she doesn't want to follow through with her diet.

For Bruzzone, breaking the taboo of the dictatorship as a serious political subject is necessary for him to be able to approach it.

"When I wrote 76, I was much more irresponsible than now, because now I know more about the historical process," he said. "With time, I learnt which words to use, and what is their meaning within this universe. Do I say 'war'? Do I say 'compensation'?"

When he mentions the word "compensation" in Smoking Under Water, he does so through the story of a relationship that the main character has with a woman who tells him that he should not accept the government's compensation, because that is what a sell-out would do. But Bruzzone explains that there are no rules when it comes to overcoming such trauma.

"For us who were affected, what is at stake is our survival. Because we are survivors," he said.

He accepted compensation, using it to build his home.

"It was very healing to be able to build a house for your family, for your children. Obviously, it doesn't fix anything – some things are insurmountable – but it works as a sort of reparation," said Bruzzone, who has three children.

He is a dissident voice who has been critical

For us who were affected, what is at stake is our survival. Because we are survivors

ABOVE: The writer Félix Bruzzone, whose parents were disappeared during Argentina's military dictatorship

of governments' responses to the human rights abuses carried out during the dictatorship.

"As a child, you need to know what happened and who did it," he said. Although trials have taken place, and most military officials are on trial or in jail, many families are still waiting for an answer.

Smoking Under Water started as a literary experiment. Bruzzone wanted to write his autobiography in three pages, but at some point he noticed a common thread: the main character smokes cigarettes, then weed, then other drugs. The character represents an entire generation that does the same: they smoke, alongside – and perhaps in part to help bear – the burdens of the past. In Argentine Spanish, *fumar* (to smoke) also means to put up with something and the story plays on this double meaning of the verb.

Even though it is told in the first person, and relates just one experience, it represents a journey through Argentina's history since the military coup in 1976: the silence during the dictatorship; the return to democracy in 1983 with the push towards justice for the victims; the shallow economic bonanza of the 1990s, with big investments and fancy yachts. The character jumps from one phase to another until he comes up with a great invention that gives him access to freedom – he can buy a yacht and sail around the world with his family while smoking waterproof cigarettes. But then comes the inevitable reflection on everything that his generation had to put up with or, as an Argentine might say, smoke. ⊗

Irene Caselli is a journalist at The Correspondent. She lives between Argentina and Italy

---

Smoking Under Water

By Félix Bruzzone

IN MARCH '76, Dad disappeared. In August, I was born, on the 23rd. And in November, two days before my cousin Lola (whom I married at the age of 27) was born, Mum disappeared. My Uncle Hugo, Lola's dad, says that in '78, sitting in front of a recently purchased TV set, watching Argentina in the World Cup, I was already chanting: "Tin-tina, tin-tina". After that, and before I got married, several things happened.

My grandma (Mum's mum, the one who brought me up) got me a grant for the private school where I went to kindergarten, elementary and high school. During that time, too, several things happened.

When I was in third grade my grandma sent me to a psychologist who, when I asked at one of the first sessions if he knew what my parents had died of, told me to ask at home. And my grandma, who until that moment had said she would tell me when I was bigger, told me. So, by third grade I was already big. One day the psychologist said to me: "I have a boat; would you like to learn to sail?" "Yes," I said, and we sailed together for almost four years. During all that time, as well as thinking about the sad fate that had befallen my parents, I came to be friends with

my psychologist's son and with another boy whose parents had also disappeared, and who came sailing with us. One summer, his grandma rented a house by the beach and he invited me and my grandma to go and stay with them. This was before I'd started high school.

Not long after that, my psychologist died and I never went sailing again. Going to his funeral was like going to Dad's, except that he had another son and wasn't really my father.

At high school I switched groups and made new friends, and because they all smoked, I learned to smoke too. My grandma told me not to at first: she said it was bad for me and that girls would notice me regardless. But I did smoke and in the end she didn't mind.

On Saturday nights I used to go to a friend's who always threw parties at his house. He lived with his mum (who travelled a lot) and his three sisters. No one knew who his dad was. He was alive, but I think my friend would have preferred him dead. Over time we drank the cellar dry and smoked all the cartons of cigarettes his mum brought back from her travels. Once, one of his sisters gave me a kiss and I fell in love. But I got over it: she kissed everyone.

When I was in fifth grade, my uncle Hugo gave me a tenor sax. I'd wanted one for a long time but because no one ever had any money to spare I'd resigned myself to never having one. I took

---

Going to his funeral was like going to Dad's, except that he had another son and wasn't really my father

---

a few lessons and before long I'd joined a funk band. It was strange: no one in the band smoked. They just drank whisky and snorted cocaine. So, I started doing that too and had some intense moments. One night, at the interval, we acted out a scene from Goodfellas in the toilets. I hadn't seen the film; now, whenever I see it, I find that scene really funny. Lola always asks me what I'm laughing at and, because she doesn't know very much about that part of my past, I never tell her anything. Then the band split up. The bass player's girlfriend got pregnant and he decided to change his life. The day he left, completely sober (which was a surprise) he said the word "priorities" over ten times. That stayed with me. Unlike him, I had no priorities. True, I had to study, so my grandma said, but I either couldn't or wouldn't, I don't know. In any case, studying wasn't my priority.

So there I was, with no priorities, until one day, on a TV show, I saw that the children of some disappeared persons had formed an organisation. My first thought was to call my friend from my sailing days. My grandma told me he was living with a friend now. I called. Before hanging up, his friend said: "My boyfriend's not here." A few months went by. One afternoon, finally, I visited the Hijos headquarters on Calle Venezuela. I found out more about what they were doing and, although none of the activities interested me all that much, I stayed.

→ What really interested me most was Gaby. Her parents hadn't disappeared; she was there because she liked helping. She was also an expert marijuana smoker, something I didn't know much about, but about which she ended up teaching me everything. We smoked together and I felt good. Sometimes, after the meetings, we'd head down to the waterfront park; we'd kiss and go into the nature reserve as far as the river, and if it was hot, we'd splash about barefoot in the mud. It was absurd, but Gaby, whose parents hadn't disappeared, was capable of doing anything to get me more involved. But I don't know if her dedication to Hijos was on my account; I suppose not.

It was also around that time that I first heard about the compensation that the government was going to hand out. I wasn't sure whether I should apply but, once I did, Gaby, who was against it all, left me. Tough luck, I thought: she might call it "crumbs", but for me it could come in handy. When I received the bonds they gave me I sold them and, not knowing what to do, I spent my time going out with the two or three remaining friends I had from high school. We had a good time, but I always had the feeling something was missing.

One night, in a bar, I met Vero. My grandma liked Vero: she had simple ideas, she didn't smoke and, because she was a vegetarian, they would talk together about the diets my grandma had to

---

There came a time when we started to lose our minds. I think I nearly lost mine forever. Vero really did lose hers: she joined a group of Zapatistas and I never heard from her again

---

go on because of her heart problems. Vero liked to travel, too, so we travelled a lot and, one day, in Palenque, in southern Mexico, we discovered a way of smoking that we both loved. And it sure was powerful. Days went by and we were in paradise. But there came a time when we started to lose our minds. I think I nearly lost mine forever. Vero really did lose hers: she joined a group of Zapatistas and I never heard from her again.

Back home and with little to lose, I went to the bank. The investment officer offered me a plot somewhere new, in a private development with a marina and golf course, and he showed me some photos: blue water, green grass, all the things that reminded me of my sailing days. I accepted, and everything was fine until I took possession of the land and realised I'd been duped: the earth was useless, and to replenish it I'd have to use so much topsoil that I'd end up spending more on that than I had buying the plot of land. Nevertheless, while I waited for prices to rise so I could sell it and make some profit, I took care to make it as serviceable as I could. So I bought a spade and a wheelbarrow and lugged topsoil for months. At that time I wanted to quit smoking, but I couldn't. I guess the effort of to-ing and fro-ing with a wheelbarrow prevents the giving up of vices.

Then, because I still had some money left over and didn't want to get conned again, I took advice from some people I trusted and eventually met Sergio, a friend who'd designed some nappies for dogs. "It's a bit of a secret," he told me, and said he still had to apply for the patents and find investors to produce them on a large scale. So I paid for the patents and we sat down to wait.

The following year, my Uncle Hugo told me that Lola, who had studied economics, had met some young entrepreneurs from overseas on a student exchange who were looking to invest in a project like ours. This was our chance. Lola, whom I hadn't seen since her fifteenth birthday, put me in touch with them, and after a few conversations we agreed that my friend and I would receive a cut from every sale. Lola was excited by the careless, confident, indifferent way I handled the negotiations. Even to this day she still thinks I had it all scrupulously planned: every stress, every slight twitch of the fingers. And, truth be told, it didn't take me long, either, to fall in love with that young businesswoman. Everything went well. In my love life: marriage to Lola and the birth of our first child. In my business life: Lola helped me sell my land and with that, along with the earnings from our venture with Sergio, we bought a flat in Puerto Madero, a sailing boat, a mooring and a little coupé so I could visit my grandma until the day when, having forgotten her diets, saying: "I'd rather live well," she died from a massive heart attack. And Sergio carried on with his inventions, all of them useless, but that one way or another made us dream of things that really were important.

Until one day, at the flat, smoking out on the terrace (the river on one side, the docks and Lola's favourite restaurants on the other), it started to rain and I suddenly imagined (I still can't explain how: Sergio was the inventor in our group) a cigarette that would stay alight in the rain. The lights from the city, from the edge of the city, reflected in the water: in the rain, the river and the docks. The mere thought of being able to lean on the balcony smoking and getting wet filled me with excitement. A special additive for the tobacco, a wrapping that was like the paper, but waterproof. He developed it; I helped him. It took us nearly two years, and a few days before the birth of my second child everything was ready. The investors (Lola always did her job well) took no time to appear. Cigarettes for smoking in the rain. That sure was an invention. So from then on, with everything finally in place, all that remained was to plan a happy future. Now, for example, I want to spruce up the boat (better kit, stronger sails) to take my family on a trip around the world. And, yes, during the trip, one rainy night, when everyone's asleep, to go out on deck, light one of those cigarettes we invented and remember, as I smoke, everything that happened. Yes, to think about it a lot. And about just how much the young people of my generation, in all that time, smoked.

*Translated by **William Gregory***

***Félix Bruzzone** is an award-winning writer from Argentina. He was named one of the 10 most important writers in the country by the newspaper Clarín*

Between the gavel and the anvil

Libyan novelist **Najwa Bin Shatwan** talks to **Orna Herr** about being arrested and accused of writing against the state. Plus an exclusive short story of hers published below

49(01): 86/93 I DOI: 10.1177/0306422020917091

"**EVEN IF THE** political system changes, the suffocating social system remains the same. The state monitors as a duty and the people monitor voluntarily."

This was how award-winning Libyan novelist Najwa Bin Shatwan summed up the current situation for writers in Libya.

Despite the death, in 2011, of hardline leader Muammar Qaddafi, censorship imposed on Libyans by the authorities, and by each other, has not disappeared.

Bin Shatwan has personal experience of this. She has written three novels and several short stories, and it was for her short story His Excellency, the Eminence of the Void, that Bin Shatwan was arrested and accused of writing against the state.

"Every bitter experience I lived has benefitted me and made me stronger in one way or another," she told Index.

Because the authorities were alerted by a member of the Libyan cultural community, Bin Shatwan says she now does not trust or consult anyone other than herself about her writing.

Female writers, she says, suffer greatly at the hands of both social and legal authorities: "A woman writer is always caught between the gavel of power and the anvil of society."

Although feminism is not directly discussed in the story, Bin Shatwan's descriptions of

female writers specifically being subject to societal censorship in Libya suggests a woman writing is a revolutionary act.

And she says it is the strength and courage to reinforce her defences in the face of such pressure that is reflected in her story The Fish Market.

The story, published below, tells of an unnamed female writer harassed by her neighbours who want her to change the details that she has written. They see themselves mirrored unflatteringly in the characters, or not mentioned at all.

The writer descends into paranoia and isolation, making changes to her story she believes her neighbours will demand, and staying locked in her home to avoid further harassment.

When the militia arrives to arrest the writer for not referring to it as a national army, her neighbours plot to erase their involvement. There are echoes of book-burning in the neighbours' plan – a practice reminiscent of oppressive governments physically destroying ideas.

Asked if the behaviour of the neighbours represented a lack of solidarity with writers in Libya who put themselves at risk, Bin Shatwan said: "I do not feel the presence of solidarity in the first place. Arab societies made us get used to the idea that once an educated woman writer gets in trouble, everyone will start attacking her."

She adds that writing in Libya "requires eluding the state and people in several ways".

Knowing she could not express herself freely in her home country, Bin Shatwan left Libya in 2012 to study for a PhD in Rome.

Two of her novels, The Horses' Hair, "which talks about the story of creation as I imagined it", and the more recently published The Slave Yards, which deals with slavery in Benghazi, will be published in English this year. ⊗

RIGHT: The author Najwa Bin Shatwan

Orna Herr is editorial assistant at Index

The Fish Market

Najwa Bin Shatwan

OUR NEIGHBOUR'S DAUGHTER wrote a story that was broadcast on the radio; we didn't hear it ourselves, but the neighbours heard it, and waited out on the street for us to return so they could tell us about it.

We had been at al-Bankina market that morning buying fish, examining the different types, and asking the fishermen about the prices, and fish of all kinds replied to our questions, because the fishermen are often drunkards and liars.

We asked them: were they fresh, or not? Had they been injured by the dynamite used to catch them? Had they nipped at the flesh of migrants, historically or recently?

The fish told us "no" by shaking their tails, and "yes" by closing their eyes. None ever lied or gave the wrong answer!

And after that, how could one believe what people say?

We took the fish home in a bag, and they listened intently to the story about al-Bankina that our neighbour #6 told. Like us, they could hardly believe that our neighbour was speaking about the same al-Bankina from which we had just returned; even the cuttlefish itself gaped in shock and astonishment, and from its mouth emerged secrets of the deep seas, mixed with a bit of our sewers, while the wrasse gave its last wriggle as the story was told.

It was the story that killed it...

Of course not, it was the writer!

And after what we heard, we were no better off than our fish; the writer had tested our patience and stoked our anger. She mentioned neighbour #7 in the story, but skipped over us, and neighbour #4, and neighbour #5, and neighbour #6 (the one who lives on the roof of house #5, and who told us the entire tale).

Why had the writer excluded us all, instead mentioning a neighbour who shamelessly wears secondhand clothes, whose body survives on rotting vegetables, and who showers with Yugoslavian shampoo?

So I approached this writer, on behalf of everyone angered by her story (which we greatly disliked), and knocked on her door. The doorbell looked at me with deep respect and asked: What do you want, Sir?

I looked at it crossly and spat at it, and it got frightened and fell quiet; I think its voice withered in that moment and hasn't grown back since.

After I'd knocked several times with my hands and feet, making a crack in the door which let in the light and revealed the left half of the writer's torso, she finally opened the door.

Writers' houses are fragile as soon as you treat them with a bit of strength. She emerged drenched in words, and could hardly pay attention to anything; of course that was nothing

→ new. She looked at us as if peering out of a photography darkroom. In sum, she was a woman who lived in her own special capsule; otherwise, such an unnatural being would never survive in our very natural society.

I began without greeting her, just as the saying goes (though I don't know who said it): "Never give writers room to speak, because they'll convince you that you're wrong, and their words will convince you you're stupid." So, I struck first, saying:

"Why do you write about the whole neighbourhood with no mention of us, the people who offered you a helping hand time and again?"

I held a copy of the story in my fist and waved it as I spoke.

The writer replied calmly:

"The story was about our former neighbourhood, where Bankina is – that is, before they moved us here, from the water to solid earth."

"Well why didn't you mention that one neighbour gave you shoes? Even if the story is about somewhere with water, and our only relationship with water is the siphon, and the rain on the roofs in winter, why didn't you mention that someone gave you shoes?"

He was so cross I think he must have knocked on the door with his feet, because she opened it quickly

---

"Because, my friend, you gave me size 39 shoes, while the child in the story is too young to put on your shoes herself."

"What does that mean? You should change the story to fit her feet. A creative writer can adjust the story as the situation requires."

"All right, don't get angry, I'll change the story for the second printing, and take your observations into consideration."

I closed the door of animosity and my anger calmed, until I glimpsed my house above all the others in the neighbourhood, and saw my underwear spread on the balcony, flying as high as the houses like a plane with no pilot.

When I read the second printing I saw that the story had been changed, but I couldn't be bothered to read all the edits. The important thing was that the part about us was there, and the way I wanted it; the rest didn't really concern me.

But one of the neighbours took the part that didn't concern me in hand, and angrily went to the writer's house. He was so cross I think he must have knocked on the door with his feet, because she opened it quickly, as if she'd been behind the door, waiting for whoever knocked on it – or knocked it down. And his knocking was as immense as the part of the story that concerned him. →

→ The neighbour protested that the house in the story sat where his family's historic home was. The spirits of their forefathers ambled through that house and shouldn't be ignored like the souls of cats. The neighbour stressed the importance of history, and that someone should write and not be discouraged by the scarcity of readers. God would favour those who read this, and this someone must come, and then tell everyone else so they could read it, at which point, he figured, culture would spread through society like fire through hay.

Cultivating hay is important, we can't not cultivate hay.

The writer surrendered to the spittle flying from the neighbour's mouth, and promised him that she would amend the relevant paragraph in the next publication, and make the changes – not to the house he thought was their house in the story, but to the house next to it. She would take advantage of the fact that the owners of the neighbouring house had fled without mentioning that the reason they did so was because their son had joined an extremist organisation and dared to slaughter some soldiers.

And she didn't include mention of the city of Zliten, which sheltered the organisation, so the people from Zliten wouldn't hate her if they happened to read the story.

The writer made the changes requested by her neighbours, one after the next, and she also introduced changes she didn't hear requested, but that she expected and speculated she might hear from neighbours who had been displaced during the Civil War, who would surely ask her for their share of edits when they returned.

So, to save time, she considered what might be on their minds, and quickly found a suitable place for them.

She thought about Mkhenib with Mkhenib's mind, about Bouajila with Bouajila's mind, about Zarkoun with Zarkoun's mind, and about Halima with Halima's mind. She even thought about Haj al-Lavi, from whose body they had taken a final platinum piece after he breathed his last. This she did as a precautionary measure; if he hadn't used up all his seven souls, he might employ one to come back to life and surprise them.

The writer would satisfy everyone, accommodate their demands, and keep her door intact too, though it would be difficult to protect her door from their knocking hands, her face from their spittle, and her mind from their trivial concerns. But if she did, and if she stopped leaving the house through it, the door's cracks would diminish, and it would regain its character.

Last Friday we saw the writer in the mosque, and she seemed serene. Since it was the first time she'd appeared there, we assumed she came to repent before God for what she had written. Everyone was filled with the same emotion, as if they had all eaten and been poisoned by the same toxic rabbitfish that was available in Bankina – all except for an old woman, who had apparently been poisoned by something else, and who burst out cursing the author!

Everyone rushed to the mosque's walls and columns to support themselves, for fear that what the old woman said would weaken their knees:

"In your story you said that I'm toothless, and that I soak my bread before chewing it. Curse you! Do I seem toothless to you?"

"Of course not... I wasn't describing you in my story, dear Hajja. Who convinced you that this character is you, and those teeth are yours?"

"Well it sounded like me, down to the last detail. You described a greying old woman, her teeth falling out, who conscientiously performs her prayers in the mosque, wears traditional clothing, and uses a cane. You wrote all that and think I won't recognise myself in your story?!"

From her breast, the old woman took the part of the story she had clipped and waved it around like conclusive evidence.

A coin and a Nokia 1011 mobile also fell from her breast, and the writer handed these back to her, saying:

"Don't be angry, dear Hajja. How should I change this central character so that it won't upset you, and won't make you complain, when your grandson reads you the story, that you're the inspiration? Help me out, and tell me how?"

The old woman rubbed her nose so hard she jostled herself. She stared into the writer's eyes for

---

It would be difficult to protect her door from their knocking hands, her face from their spittle, and her mind from their trivial concerns

---

several seconds, then said humbly:

"Since you want my opinion, you can make an old woman in the story resemble Um al-Khair. She's also an old woman who performs her prayers, whose teeth are falling out, and no one in the neighbourhood knows her. Even if you write that she's Um al-Khair, like this in bold, no one will know it's her. Try it... try it. Writing is very freeing and liberating."

"Oh, dear Hajja! The work can't handle me inserting another character into it."

"Why not? Successful writers can make room for new events or unexpected characters to appear in a story. Where two can sit, so can three. You're a great devil; you can fill a six-person bus with a hundred and one passengers."

"And who's number one hundred and one?"

"Oh I don't know! You know... you're a great all-knowing devil: you wrote that Um al-Saad is heating by getting two salaries from the state. You knew about the two salaries, so how hard can it be for you to figure out the final passenger? And why so jealous? My husband dies and I inherit his pension, then Ibn Barr gave me his position in parliament, another salary for being the candidate's mother? These character traits have been carefully studied, you can't have just put them into the story by chance, so stop messing around. You don't yet know Um al-Saad Deghm."

→ The old woman calmed down, and everyone relaxed their hands from the columns and walls they had embraced, except for one person, who rediscovered comfort in the column, so his prayer was embracing the column.

The third printing:

On Sunday, the writer entered her house, carrying the new edition to which she had made the necessary changes to appease her angry neighbours. She found her neighbours who had returned from displacement sitting in her mother's living room. The writer asked:

"Mother, what happened?"

Each one of them had dictated to her mother the changes they wanted made to the story. And their requests successively accumulated on the table, where Becky the housecat was sleeping underneath.

The story became completely different; the writer needed a wheeled cart to transport these from the salon to the basement where she secluded herself to write.

She stood in front of the table of requests with her hands behind her back, the way Beethoven did when music played in his mind that his ears could not hear. And if Becky hadn't suddenly leapt down to the basement in a panic at the violent knocking at the front door, the writer wouldn't have sensed what was going on around her.

"Open up, quick! Open up, if you don't we'll bring the house down on your heads!" called a voice from outside.

One of the neighbours opened the door, since the writer's door now belonged to everyone, free of charge. Al-Kani militia entered, and grabbed the writer by her clasped arms. They recognised her from the position of her hands, but the writer didn't pay attention to them... she kept gazing at the papers on the table and the requests flowing out of them... and she floated along with where they took her, as if moving to the beat of traditional Libyan music, whose rhythm no one can escape.

One of them said:

"She mentioned the militia in her story verbatim, and didn't call them a national army, so she was arrested."

Another said:

"That's exactly what she did. Al-Kani militia is a bunch of bandits and criminals."

Another:

"The Seventh Brigade took her to an unknown location."

Another:

"Psshhh... there's no such thing as an 'unknown location', Libya's a small country."

Another:

"We must deny having anything to do with the story and its writer, and get rid of the requests for edits immediately, before the militia searches the basement. And by that we mean the Seventh Brigade, God forgive us."

Another:

"What should we do?"

Another:

"Make the sewers flood the basement."

Another:

"No, not the sewers. Sewers flooded a bank before, and damaged the money deposited there. The sewers themselves don't have a plan, until you use them twice, with the bank and then the basement. No, I'm begging you, forget about the sewers; that's already been done often enough."

Another:

"What you're saying is true; the river of sewage can't be unleashed twice, we have to change tactics: to burning."

Another:

"Let's burn down the basement."

Everyone whispered:

"Good idea. Let's burn down the basement."

For the first time in the history of stories, a story cried over its characters and plot, and short and long stories of the world heard how she moaned:

"No one can finish me off. I'll be honest with you, I hate you all, everyone who put your characters inside me. I'll expose you all and say that everyone whose names and characters appear in the story are identical to reality, not simply a coincidence."

The story cried extensively, and Becky suffocated in the basement. Then a week came in which old Um al-Saad Deghm was appointed cultural attaché to Egypt, and the United Nations considered Libya's sewers to be an environmental danger, which should be put under international protection.

Then a week passed in which nothing happened, and the fish in al-Bankina were so shocked, so astounded, that they figured there must be some kind of conspiracy.

The writer, however, has been taken to a psychiatric hospital and is currently undergoing electroshock therapy in good hands.

Her treatment is free, though the electricity is costly.

Translated by **Elisabeth Jaquette**

Najwa Bin Shatwan *is an award-winning Libyan academic and writer. She has written three novels, a collection of short stories, plays and contributions to anthologies*

We could all disappear

Bangladeshi writer **Neamat Imam** talks to **Jemimah Steinfeld** about his new novel, which looks at the real-life disappearance of a writer in his country in the 1970s

49(01): 94/98 I DOI: 10.1177/0306422020917092

LEFT: The writer Neamat Imam, whose first book on Bangladesh has yet to find a publisher in the country due to its criticisms of the government

IF IT'S IMPOSSIBLE to discover the truth behind the disappearance of a prominent and celebrated writer, could we all just disappear? This is the question that preoccupies Neamat Imam, himself a celebrated writer.

The author of two books, one of which will be released later this year, the Bangladesh-born writer is now working on his third, with an excerpt published below. This novel looks at the real-life disappearance of one of the most important writers from Bangladesh, Zahir Raihan, who went missing in 1972 at the age of 36. Raihan disappeared shortly after he released a documentary, Stop Genocide, which was made during the Bangladesh Liberation War. Imam believes that Raihan was likely to have unreleased footage showing Bangladesh in a bad light and that was, perhaps, behind his disappearance and presumed murder.

"How secure am I?" is a central question which Imam says he is addressing in the book.

"People disappear all the time in Bangladesh," he added, explaining that today people censor themselves a lot and the whole society lives in fear. Over the decades, he says, the state has created a number of tools that control people.

But there are other questions, as the extract shows. The book imagines what might have happened to Raihan through a series of fictionalised characters who, in this instance, assassinate him in what Imam says is a moment of "political madness". Following their cover-up of the crime, they are exiled into a world of silence where they can't discuss the truth. Their guilt eats away at them just as the rats, in one part of the book, eat at their feet.

"When we talk about an assassination, we talk about who is killed and who has killed... but we do not actually understand what goes through the mind of the assassin after the crime has happened," said Imam.

"If you think about the Saudi dissident Jamal Khashoggi, who has been killed in Istanbul, we know that five people have been sentenced to death in Saudi Arabia, but do we know what is going to happen to the people who have actually masterminded the killing? We don't know; we'll never know."

Originally from a remote part of Bangladesh, Imam encountered his first newspaper at the age of 14, when his elder brother returned with a weekend supplement. Imam was immediately transfixed.

"That newspaper was a kind of invitation to me from the world beyond."

Imam got his brother to bring back a newspaper every weekend, and from that moment he developed a thirst to know as much as possible.

This thirst eventually led him to university in the capital, Dhaka, (something frowned upon by his brother at the time, who thought that such a path was "spoilt") and then abroad.

But his quest for knowledge has come at a cost. Imam now lives in a form of self-imposed

Do we know what is going to happen to the people who have actually masterminded the killing? We don't know; we'll never know

exile in Canada. His award-winning 2014 book, The Black Coat, was a bold and critical look at the early years of Bangladesh.

"It was very political, and Bangladesh is not a good place for writers who want to speak their mind," he said.

Imam has not been back to Bangladesh since the book was released.

"I am very afraid of my life because even bloggers are not very free in Bangladesh. It made international headlines that one American blogger was chopped [up] with a machete, in Bangladesh," he said, referencing Avijit Roy, an American-Bangladeshi online activist who was murdered in 2015. Roy was one of several writers in Bangladesh who have been killed in recent years for taking a less orthodox stance

(see Summer 2015, 44.02, p76-77).

Unsurprisingly, in a country where publishers can also find themselves at the wrong end of the machete, The Black Coat has yet to find a publisher there – a great sadness for Imam.

"This book is not for the world; it is for Bangladeshis," he said. Does Imam have any hope about his country and his writing prospects there? Despite it all, he does.

"I believe that one day it will be published and a new government will come. Or maybe, one day soon, someone will take a chance."

ABOVE: Renowned Bangladeshi activist, film director and writer Zahir Raihan, who disappeared in 1972

Jemimah Steinfeld is deputy editor of Index on Censorship magazine

---

For The Sake of Future Books

Neamat Imam

EARLY IN THE morning of the seventh day of his incarceration, the three operatives of the New Leadership appeared before novelist Zahir Raihan with a rusty metal pail of regular size. They were as sleepless as he was and, probably, as much under pressure from the authority as he was to successfully complete their task. They placed his head within the pail and then struck the pail constantly with a random stick, causing booming reverberations. This had been done before, at least twice, and for over six hours each time, in between burning his torso with a heated iron rod and crushing his scrotum with a hand-painted glass bottle, but somehow they still believed this would work on him on the third go, as they had seen their latest method of torture – immersing his head into water contaminated with urine and faeces – to have no fruitful impact on him.

They took turns with the stick, removed the pail from Zahir Raihan's head, menacingly asked him a few questions, and violently placed the pail on him again when he refused to answer to them at all or provided them an answer that they were not satisfied with. At about 8 o'clock, after eating a swift breakfast and with a cup of tea standing right before him, they blindfolded him with a black cloth to transfer him from the darkened underground apartment to a white van idling about an hour in the front yard of the building. In the soft light of day, their eyes stopped

CREDIT: Wenshu He

momentarily on his sprained wrists, his busted lips, the restraint markings on his neck and the bruises on his arms. But the moment of taking a final decision about him had arrived for them, and they had no time to waste. Quietly, they drove through narrow neighbourhood streets that were strewn with litter and a mess of garbage, and accelerated once they reached the high street, to transport him to Burman House in the centre of the city.

Although the operatives had constantly deprived him of food and drink up to that point, and they had subjected him to an extraordinary amount of torture, to hand over to them the rumoured manuscript of his new novel, Stop Genocide, Zahir Raihan did not show any sign of cracking up. Instead, he maintained his usual graciousness and moved with a supremely pronounced air of dignity that was only possible for a person of his stature. He honestly believed his highest treasure in life was his own mind and he would, under no circumstances, permit anyone to pollute or poison it. He faced his visitors with great patience and reiterated to them boldly, as he had done innumerable times before in the past few days, that there existed no such manuscript that he was hiding from them, and that he would not have hidden it by any means had he written one, even

---

As far as he knew, it was a manuscript that could not fall into the hands of the public in its present form, he said; if it did, it would undermine anything and everything that New Leadership stood for

---

if he believed he would be considered fiercely disloyal to the authority for doing so. He had difficulty speaking, but he managed to lift his face and say concretely that he was very clear about his expectation from himself as well as from those around him: there was no need to ask him the same questions again and again.

One of his visitors was Dr Karim Chaudhury. Dr Chaudhury was deeply disturbed by Zahir Raihan's non-cooperation regarding the manuscript. He had coordinated his abduction and incarceration so far, although he had been a friend of his since their high school days together, and now he needed to come to a conclusion about him. He came forward in a few reluctant steps to request Zahir Raihan for the last time to change his mind. Zahir Raihan would definitely undergo further incarceration, he said with extreme irritation, and he may even be tortured to death, if he did not hand over the manuscript to the authority. As far as he knew, it was a manuscript that could not fall into the hands of the public in its present form, he said; if it did, it would undermine anything and everything that New Leadership stood for and that the revolution was about. Because of his long contribution to the revolution, he said, there was a slim possibility that Zahir Raihan

→ would be banished, instead of being killed, to the island of St Martin's in the Bay of Bengal for the rest of his life. But he was not sure how that would be of any help to Zahir Raihan in achieving what he wanted to achieve by going against the authority. "St Martin's is full of venomous pit vipers and saltwater crocodiles," he said, "not many people I know of survived there more than a few hours."

When Dr Karim Chaudhury's intense effort resulted in mere silence on the part of Zahir Raihan, Manobika Raihan, Zahir Raihan's third wife and a prominent businesswoman, was called into the room.

A valuable member of the inner core of the New Leadership, she was, in fact, the first person to alert the authority about the existence of Zahir Raihan's manuscript. To assist Dr Chaudhury in his interrogation, she abruptly ended her long, confrontational telephonic conversation with someone from New Leadership's central command, and, stepping ahead of Dr Chaudhury, began by commenting that Zahir Raihan had a dark soul, one that was darker than the soul of any enemy of the New Leadership she was aware of. He was an emotionless and complicated person, she said, and she had known it from the beginning that it would not be easy to extract any information from him regarding the manuscript. His writing had poisoned their conjugal life, she claimed; she would forgive him for that, but she was determined to accept any amount of hardships to help New Leadership govern the country without distraction. She wanted Zahir Raihan to reconsider his position for his own sake and for the sake of the many beautiful books he could write in the future if he remained alive.

Zahir Raihan lifted his face to speak to them. "I'm an author," he said. "I'm an author and if I write a book it means that that book is long overdue in the world. Nothing more. Nothing less."

Neamat Imam is a Bangladeshi-Canadian author of literary fiction. His first novel, The Black Coat, became A Quill & Quire Book of the Year, and a CBC Best Canadian Debut Novel of the Year, in 2016

Demand points of view

Graduates of Index's Free Speech Is For Me programme tell **Orna Herr** why they grabbed the chance to chat to people with opposing views

49(01): 99/101 I DOI: 10.1177/0306422020917093

" **I THINK WE NEED** to re-understand it, re-articulate it, re-defend it so that it becomes inculcated into our culture at a deeper level once again," said Inaya Folarin Iman, project leader of Index's Free Speech Is For Me programme, talking about free speech.

Free Speech Is For Me is Index's training and mentoring programme which, so far, has worked with 13 advocates from the UK and the USA.

Iman became passionate about free speech during her time as features editor on the Leeds University student newspaper. After graduating, she wanted to continue to advocate "especially as someone from a background where you don't traditionally hear from people who look like me. Being a young woman of African heritage, I really wanted to be part of the voices that are broadening the debate on free speech".

UK advocate Ash Kotak, an award-winning playwright, told Index about his personal experiences of censorship.

He said: "I wrote a gay, romantic comedy called Hijra [published in 2000] and I had dreadful attacks from my community, just because it was gay... people in the South Asian community felt I'd let down the community because I was talking about these issues.

"I think it's very healthy to have a different point of view, but [also to] know why. That's what I think a lot of people would have got from the [Free Speech Is For Me] programme."

Rhiannon Adams, a fellow UK advocate, also came to the programme following personal experiences of censorship. She faced trolling when she became vocal online about women's issues. She said: "I was pretty young at the time and I didn't have any idea how to deal with it. It felt so invasive and it really just shut me down.

"We had the training on self-care online, about trolling and how to deal with it [as part of the Free Speech Is For Me programme]. I thought that was really helpful, having the tools to be able to step forward on some issues and not feel scared to be challenged on them."

RIGHT: Members of the current youth advisory board

ABOVE: Matthew Caruana Galizia (second to right), son of late journalist Daphne Caruana Galizia, at the Sued into Silence conference in Amsterdam in February with (from left to right) Sarah Clarke, Charlie Holt and Caoilfhionn Gallagher

→ Another graduate of the programme, Max Lane, told Index he sometimes felt he was not "allowed" to talk about subjects he wanted to debate: "It's not always laws or rules or a student union, it's kind of a feeling. It's the vibe you get on campus."

Of the Free Speech Is For Me session, he said: "It felt like the most open university seminar that I've ever been to. It was quite liberating."

US advocate Maya Rubin, a student at Wellesley College, in Massachusetts, also felt strongly about university campuses and classrooms being places where ideas could be freely exchanged. She said: "Self-censorship is the most frequent and pernicious way in which free inquiry is stifled on campuses."

She added that the Free Speech Is For Me programme had left her "more prepared to educate others about the movement".

Another US advocate, Obden Mondésir, said that while many considered the First Amendment to the US constitution (which includes the right to free speech) as key to how the country developed, he felt that honouring the 14th Amendment (which grants citizenship to anyone born or naturalised in the USA) as a result of the civil rights movement was vital in the fight for free speech of minorities.

"Using the First Amendment as a tool that … really supports what the 14th Amendment is all about, I feel like that was the first time you had a country that actually supports all the citizens that are born in that nation."

Another project Index is currently conducting is research into the nature and frequency of vexatious actions against journalists, known as "strategic lawsuits against public participation" (Slapps). This is being run by policy researcher

and advocacy officer Jessica Ní Mhainín. These actions include letters threatening legal action for libel and defamation with the aim to silence journalists.

Ní Mhainín said: "It comes down to abuse of power."

Slapps are often used by corporations or wealthy individuals, sometimes targeting freelance journalists who lack the resources to fight back and find themselves censored as a result.

She said that the sexism faced by female journalists could also come into play when looking at Slapps. Matthew Caruana Galizia, son of the journalist Daphne Caruana Galizia, spoke about his mother at the Sued into Silence conference in Amsterdam in February. He said that his mother, who had 42 civil suits against her at the time of her death, was targeted partly because she was a woman speaking out against men.

The project is being conducted now, Ní Mhainín said, because "some of the most recent examples of Slapps are also some of the most aggressive ones… You almost have to have eyes in the back of your head to see who might be coming for you".

Censorship of the press often manifests itself in the form of legislation against media freedom. But, as the Slapps project shows, it also comes from within societies. This is the case with censorship of the arts.

Index deputy editor Jemimah Steinfeld attended the Human International Documentary Film Festival in Oslo in February and spoke about how far-right sections of society are focused on restricting artistic freedoms.

She identified that, while leaders such as Brazil's President Jair Bolsonaro and prime minister of Hungary Viktor Orbán impacted artistic expression by dictating the use of artistic and educational funds, this was not the sole source of censorship.

Speaking after the event she told Index: "We're seeing many people, especially on the right, who are more emboldened to protest (sometimes violently) against art and culture they don't like." But she insisted that it was vital to allow people on both sides of the political spectrum to express themselves artistically.

She said the defence of artistic expression meant "allowing the far right to be able to express themselves artistically. One of the arguments that is coming up time and again across countries and cultures is this sense that the arts are dominated by the left and that there is no room for other voices".

"A vibrant art scene is one in which all kinds of voices, even those we don't agree with, have room to speak and perform," she added.

To discuss issues such as this, Index has recently recruited a new youth board of eight people between the ages of 16 and 25 from around the world, who gather online each month for an exchange of ideas. The board includes two members from India, who can bring first-hand accounts of life since the citizenship law was brought in under Prime Minister Narendra Modi's government in December 2019. This has sparked protests as it is deemed to discriminate against Muslims.

Samarth Mishra, from the central Indian city of Gwalior, said: "The student protests across the country against the government are just a sign that the youth is critical, and it doesn't make them anti-national. Instead of attacking the higher education institute's students, the government should try to be open to criticism and listen to their concerns."

The board also includes members from Sweden, Canada and Hong Kong, as well as the UK, promising a fascinating series of discussions on international freedom of expression issues.

Index's Freedom of Expression Awards will take place in London at the May Fair Hotel on 30 April. The ceremony marks the 20th anniversary of the awards.

There are 15 nominees over four categories: digital activism, campaigning, arts and journalism. One nominee in the journalism category is the Hong Kong Free Press, which was founded in 2015 with the aim to be the

You almost have to have eyes in the back of your head to see who might be coming for you

most trustworthy independent English-language news source in the region.

In a statement published on the outlet's website, Tom Grundy, co-founder and editor-in-chief, said: "We are grateful to be considered for this award and am proud of our team for building a much-needed, independent platform at a time when press freedom is under increasing pressure."

Nominees in the digital activism category include Egypt-based HarrassMap, who campaign against sexual harassment, and 7amleh, who focus on protecting the human rights of Palestinians.

Nominees in the arts category include Russian LGBTQ activist Yulia Tsvetkova and Thai rap group Rap Against Dictatorship, while the campaigning category includes Prove They Are Alive!, an organisation that campaigns against forced disappearances in Turkmen prisons. ⊗

Orna Herr is the Tim Hetherington fellow 2020 at Index

LEFT: Playwright Ash Kotak and Rhiannon Adams, UK advocates of Index's Free Speech is for Me programme

Ticking the boxes

While elections are being cancelled due to coronavirus, **Jemimah Steinfeld** reviews how grassroots groups have been facing opposition to their attempts to get more people to vote

49(01): 102/104 I DOI: 10.1177/0306422020917094

THERE APPEARS TO be no end to what the Ugandan state will do to reduce the influence of People Power, a political movement set up by singer Bobi Wine.

At the end of February, Rita Nabukenya, a supporter of the movement, was run over and killed by a police patrol truck while walking down the street in Kampala wearing People Power colours. Many believe she was hit on purpose.

"They have done everything possible to try to silence People Power," David Rukiri, Wine's political adviser, told Index. He reeled off a long list of classic intimidation tactics – tapping phones, restricting movement, banning public speaking.

Wine, who joined parliament as an independent in 2017, uses his songs as vehicles to criticise the government. For that he has been arrested and had his shows cancelled countless times. Rukiri says that, given how difficult it is to organise a rally now, the group turns up to places that it knows already have gatherings – weddings and funerals, for example – to campaign to end corruption and get out the vote.

"The regime has been really effective at creating apathy among young people," said Rukiri. "Until Bobi Wine, people – especially young people – were really detached from the political scene. They were made to think that politics was something for other people, not them.

"Bobi, who is young and interested in politics, has tried to show how politics affects them in every aspect of their lives. For example, a lack of

jobs is because of the political system. So now lots of young people want to vote in 2021. The electoral commission has registered 2.5 million new voters since 2018. The government is scared of [these] young people."

The Ugandan government might not be the only ones scared by the potential power of new voters. In the USA, there is mounting evidence of systemic attempts to prevent certain people from voting. Voter turnout has remained low there for several decades – at 58% in the 2016 presidential election, particularly among certain groups. Black voter turnout dropped by 7% in 2016.

"We're the only advanced democracy that deliberately discourages people from voting," said former US president Barack Obama in 2018.

Tennessee ranks 49th out of the 50 US states in terms of voter turnout. Hedy Weinberg, executive director of the American Civil Liberties Union of Tennessee, told Index there had been a marked increase in voter suppression efforts since 2011, when the state imposed a law requiring presentation of photo ID to vote.

"The impact will hit hardest in communities that have been historically disenfranchised and rely on voter registration drives to empower individuals and gain access to the ballot box," she said.

Laina Reynolds Levy works at VoteRiders, an organisation that helps people to get the required ID. She told Index: "The people who are affected by voter ID laws are disproportionately voters of colour, young people, older voters [who might not drive], and women if they've changed their name upon getting married.

""Our fundamental value is that every eligible voter should be able to make their voice heard, and having a restrictive ID law is a barrier to that."

The organisation's work might not sound too controversial in a country such as the USA, which prides itself on democracy, but Reynolds Levy says that every so often it is the subject of critical media.

ABOVE: A South African woman and her grandson cast her vote in the general election of May 2019. The African National Congress won with 57.5%, the lowest vote share since apartheid ended in 1994

As an organisation that deals with the disenfranchising effects of voter ID, it rubs against those who see this as an essential way to stop voter fraud (a rare occurrence). As a result, in addition to battling rumours and confusion from people about how – and where – to vote, it also encounters disinformation. In February, for example, conservative foundation Judicial Watch issued a press release before the Iowa caucus claiming that eight counties in Iowa had more voters on their registration rolls than were eligible to vote, something that Iowa's secretary of state dismissed as inaccurate.

Disinformation is one way to stop those aiding voters in their tracks; a lawsuit is another. In Tennessee, the ACLU is currently involved in a lengthy court battle with the secretary of state. The suit seeks an injunction against a law

We're the only advanced democracy that deliberately discourages people from voting

that, if passed, will come into effect on 1 October and will impose criminal and civil penalties on organisations hosting voter registration drives if they return incomplete applications or fail to comply with certain requirements.

Lawsuits – and the threat of them – make freedom of assembly and activism around elections that much harder. They seek to silence

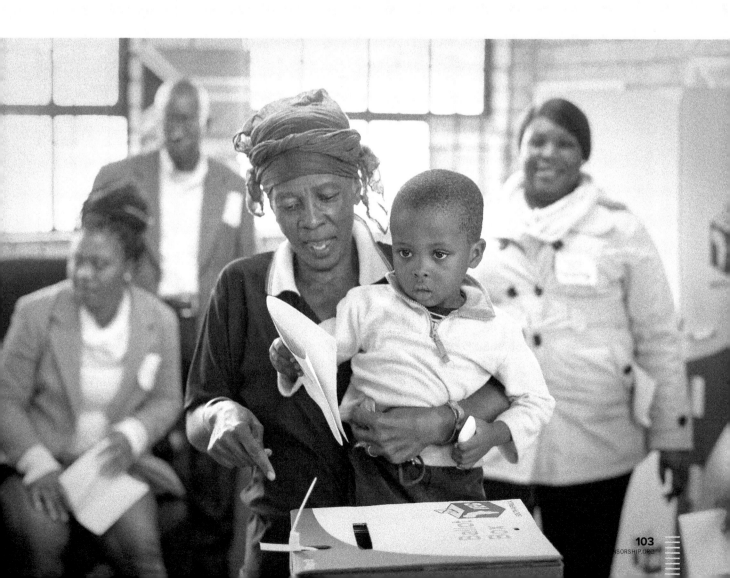

Our fundamental value is that every eligible voter should be able to make their voice heard

→ the people working hard to ensure everyone has an equal political voice on election day.

Index spoke to Poland's OKO.press, an investigative journalism and fact-checking portal, which works with activists across the country who are united in a desire to make Poland's political system more transparent and fair.

Six thousand people support it financially on a regular basis – but Poland's current right wing Law and Justice Party, in power since 2016, is not among these supporters.

"We now face a defamation lawsuit brought by a new judge of the Supreme Court, Konrad Wytrykowski," Piotr Pacewicz, editor-in-chief of OKO, told Index.

"He alleges that we insulted him [by] writing that he took part in a WhatsApp group associated with the justice ministry, whose members are believed to take part in a smear campaign on the internet against individual judges who criticise [the] government's changes to the judiciary."

Bolstered by two million unique users each month, OKO continues to work.

"We are resilient in the face of intimidation or threats, not only because of the integrity and courage of our journalists but also because we feel the support of our readers and donors," said Pacewicz.

But how many others are put off?

Like OKO, South Africa's My Vote Counts sees the best way to get people to vote is to tackle the lack of information. Sheilan Clarke, the organisation's communications officer, told Index that in the 2019 general election, South Africa recorded its lowest voter turnout since it became a democracy.

Only 66% of those registered to vote cast their ballots – an 11% decrease from 2014. Almost six million young people under the age of 30 were eligible to vote but didn't register.

Clarke said: "You can't simply just go up to someone and tell them: 'you should go vote because it's your democratic right'. You will be met with 'why?' or 'politicians don't care about me'."

"From a long-term perspective, we believe that a political system that is more transparent and accountable to the people will result in greater participation and inclusiveness, and all of our work is aimed towards this.

"We see great value in providing information that allows the electorate and the public more generally to make political choices from a more informed position, providing the tools to hold our leaders accountable."

For example, the Political Party Funding Act – which it led calls for – was signed by President Cyril Ramaphosa last year. But it has yet to be implemented because he did not sign the date of implementation, which Clarke thinks could have been intentional.

Despite the setbacks, these organisations are emerging political forces, giving a voice to millions who might otherwise feel left out.

The UK general election in December 2019 saw the emergence of Network.Vote, which wants to get the "unheard third" of voters out to the polls. In Hungary, celebrities supported an awareness campaign that encouraged Roma people to vote in the 2018 general election.

"We just had a very busy beginning of the week. Things are definitely ramping up," said Reynolds Levy, who is coming up for air after Super Tuesday, when many primaries were held in the election for the Democratic presidential candidate.

As for Bobi Wine and David Rukiri, death threats will not stop them. "We are trying to organise, organise, organise," said Rukiri. "And of course the environment is very hostile, but we tell people not to give up." ⊗

Jemimah Steinfeld *is deputy editor at Index on Censorship magazine*